SMOKING SALMON & TROUT

plus Pickling, Salting, Sausaging & Care

by Jack Whelan

Aerie Publishing

Aerie Publishing
R.R. 1, Site 156, C27
Bowser, B.C., V0R 1G0

Second Printing – August, 1983
Third Printing – September, 1984
Fourth Printing – April, 1986
Fifth Printing – July, 1987
Sixth Printing – July, 1988
Seventh Printing – April, 1990
Eighth Printing – August. 1991
Ninth Printing – March, 1993
Tenth Printing – March, 1995
Eleventh Printing – March, 1997
Twelfth Printing – March, 1998
Thirteenth Printing – January, 1999

Canadian Cataloguing in Publication Data

Whelan, Jack, 1917 -
    Smoking salmon and trout

ISBN 0-919807-00-3

1. Fishery products - Preservation. 2. Salmon.
3. Trout. I. Title.
TX612.S4W493   641.4'946   C83-091013-1

Distributed by **Gordon Soules Book
Publishers Ltd**. ● 1359 Ambleside Lane,
West Vancouver, BC, Canada V7T 2Y9
● PMB 620, 1916 Pike Place #12,
Seattle, WA 98101-1097 US
E-mail: books@gordonsoules.com
Web site: http://www.gordonsoules.com
(604) 922 6588 Fax: (604) 688 5442

Cover Design: Neil Havers, Courtenay, B.C.
Printed in Canada by Friesen Printers, Altona, Manitoba, Canada

To my skilled doctors and the dedicated staff at Royal Jubilee Hospital, Victoria. They gave me a good-as-new heart, and it supplied the renewed energy that made this book possible.

ACKNOWLEDGEMENTS

I am extremely grateful to my wife, Nancy, for doing the arduous tasks of editing and proofreading.

Thanks to John Hicks for his unselfish help in getting me started at writing this, and to my father, who by example, gave me the tenacity to finish it.

CREDITS

Illustration are by the author with the following exceptions:

Cover photo, Studio 1, Courtenay, B.C.

Inside cover, p. 81, p. 82, B.C. Provincial Museum

p. 103, Nelson Dewey

p. 106, p. 112, p. 179, p. 180, p. 183, Torry Research Station, Aberdeen, Scotland

p. 109, p. 110, United States Fish & Wildlife Service

p. 111, Fisheries & Oceans Canada

p. 112, Washington State Dept. of Fisheries

p. 181, p. 182, p. 183, p. 185, p. 188, Nancy Whelan

1
9
4
4

The Aleutian Islands during World War II was the scene of my first fish smoking attempt. There were plenty of salmon there, but the next most important ingredient - smoke - was hard to come by. There wasn't a single tree in all those desolate windswept islands. Not knowing any better, I thought that driftwood was the perfect answer. Any of you who know the pungency of driftwood smoke can guess that the first attempt wasn't noted for its success. That was in 1944 and I have no idea how many fish smoking sessions I've had since. A few of the results over the years have been fair but most fell far short of good. In recent years I've organized my efforts to get consistently better results. This preamble is about how I got that done.

I was constantly looking in local libraries, etc., for some help with my smoking process but couldn't find a lead. There just wasn't any helpful information. Of course my life then was full with raising a family, and trying to keep up with the expanding knowledge in my regular fields of endeavor.

About 15 years ago I had a memorable taste of real smoked salmon! Up to that time, all that I had experienced in the way of smoked fish was my hit and miss results and those of others who used the same approach. There was the occasional piece of smoked salmon bought at some seaside establishment, but it had the same dried up character as mine. Then there were the several exposures to Lox, but I had no idea how it was made, that being a closely guarded secret. About 15 years ago, my theretofore sheltered life began to expand. Then, at a business luncheon my host insisted that I have a "starter" of smoked salmon. He had no trouble convincing me. Dining out had always been an infrequent event, in those days, on a budget that didn't allow such expensive extras as "starters". When I tasted that smoked salmon I couldn't believe my palate - I wasn't ready for such a treat. The Maitre d'Hotel told me that it was Scotch smoked and I subsequently found that it was the only type served in fine eating places.

Not too long after that memorable introduction to Scotch Smoked salmon, I was able to travel to Ireland, Scotland, Britain and the continent. There I found not only Scotch or Irish smoked salmon, but also smoked trout and many other smoked fish on menus everywhere. I was also able to find a bit of information on smoking on the bookshelves. A few times the business schedule, that had been arranged for me, allowed time for a chat with fishmongers. A few of them sold nothing but Scotch or Irish smoked salmon, no other fish.

The following year I again visited Scotland, Ireland and Britain on business and planned to have a few days' holiday while there. That holiday allowed me to visit some fish smoking and processing plants and most importantly, spend time at the Torry Fisheries Research Laboratory at Aberdeen, Scotland. That visit was extremely rewarding for me. I was, and still am amazed at the advanced degree of technology that the fishing industry of Britain has and makes use of. A most important part of this visit was the start of my own technical library on all phases of fish processing.

Following that trip, the library research service offered by my encyclopedia, gave me a start on some American fish processing information, some of the most important of which was fish smoking work done by the Washington State Fisheries Department. This in turn led me to a wealth of information on fish processing done by the Fisheries Research Board of Canada.

With all this new knowledge to use, I soon became aware of the limitations of my smoking equipment and began to evolve a small portable smoker patterned after the large, modern fish smoking plants of Ireland, Scotland, and many European coutries. This modern smoker gave me the ability to turn out all the different smoked products with assurance of success.

Years ago, a Canadian publisher of fishing books asked me to do a book on smoking. We agreed that a report on the commercial methods of smoking, as done in various countries, was to be its theme. It was to be a resume of the information (I had found) so difficult for the home smoker in North America to find. I started on it, but found that much of the information was hard to get organized in a satisfactory way. The processes that I had worked with and adapted for home use were easy enough to write about, but there were too many things that I was simply trying to report without the necessary intimate knowledge. I needed to *try* and *perfect* all the various processes before I could write about them.

Five years ago I retired from business and moved to British Columbia. Here I had an abundant supply of raw material and now the time to really learn about fish processing. Not how the processes are done in commercial plants, but how to successfully do them at home.

Now I feel comfortable with all the processes, I can write about them with confidence. As a result I have decided to self publish the information.

While gathering smoking information I came upon other processes: pickling (marinating), salting, drying, freezing, canning, sausage-making, and fish care. So many of these intriguing processes begged to be tried, so try them I did. We found a whole new world of good eating - sometimes we enjoy fish delicacies as often as three times a day! We truly eat like royalty with little cash outlay.

My research also led to a greater satisfaction with the fish I catch, and species I must buy, because of their being better cared for. We can really see and taste the difference between my previous casual care of my catch then freezing according to ordinary instructions, and the business-like care the fish now get until they are *quick frozen.*

Just as importantly, I found how useful the old arts of salting and marinating (pickling) can be. Despite all out advanced technology, there are still times when we don't have the modern conveniences of refrigeration and freezing available. It's often just then that the best fishing is available.

Thus a book that started as a resume of fish *smoking* processes has become a collection of varied processes and recipes enjoyed by many cultures. It tells you step by step how to do all the processes so that you can be sure of an enjoyable final product. Some of the processes are applicable only to salmon and the larger trout; (for convenience, I lump the chars with the trouts because that is the way most of us carry them in our heads. Perhaps we should call them all salmonids as the biologists do).

Other processes do for any size salmon and trout, and a few relate only to the smaller fish of those species.

Some of the processes, for example: pickling or marinating, and sausages and specialty making, are appropriate for other fish as well as the salmon and trout.

Whether you like your salmon or trout prepared simply or elegantly, you will find between these covers many ways to please your palate and those of your family and friends.

I hope you enjoy using this book as much as I've enjoyed doing it for you.

CONTENTS

How to use this book

Frustration is inevitable when researching the literature for information, I have found. Some books don't even have an index. To make this book easier to use, I've tried to organize the information so that you can go straight to the thing you are looking for.

As you can see the book is divided into six parts.

Each part is divided into chapters dealing with specific divisions of that part, for example: Chapter 8 - Scotch Smoking; Chapter 11 - Making Lox. At the beginning of each of the six parts is a list of the Chapter titles which will immediately take you to the chapter you need.

At the beginning of each chapter is a list of key phrases from the various pieces of information that make up the chapter. This list tells you on which page you will find the specific bit of information you seek.

When you get to that page, the key phrase will be in bold type to further assist you.

If you have any suggestions for making things easier to find I'd be very grateful if you would write to me. It would help my future books be more useful to others. That's what a book like this is meant to be - useful.

Thanks,
Jack Whelan
R.R. # 1, Bowser, B.C.
Canada V0R 1G0

SALMON & TROUT

TROUT		Atlantic salmon	Salmo salar
	also	Landlocked salmon	Salmo salar
		Ouananiche	Salmo salar
		Brown trout	Salmo truta
		Cutthroat trout	Salmo clarki
		Rainbow trout	Salmo gairdneri
		Steelhead trout	Salmo gairdneri
	lesser known	Apache trout	Salmo apache
		Gila trout	Salmo gilae
		Golden trout	Salmo aguabonita
		Mexican golden trout	Salmo crystogaster
CHAR		Brook trout	Salvelinus fontinalus
		Lake trout	Salvelinus namaycush
	also	Bank trout	Salvelinus namaycush
		Grey trout	Salvelinus namaycush
		Mackinaw trout	Salvelinus namaycush
		Siscowet trout	Salvelinus namaycush
		Togue trout	Salvelinus namaycush
	hybrids	Splake trout	
		Tiger trout	
		Arctic char	Salvelinus alpinus
	also	Blueback trout	Salvelinus alpinus
		Sunapee trout	Salvelinus alpinus
		Dolly varden trout	Salvelinus malma
SALMON		Chinook salmon	Oncorhynchus tsawyscha
		Chum salmon	Oncorhynchus keta
		Coho salmon	Oncorhynchus kisutch
		Pink salmon	Oncorhynchus gorbuscha
		Sockeye salmon	Oncorhynchus nerka
	also	Kokanee	Oncorhynchus nerka

1
CARE OF THE CATCH & BUTCHERING FISH

CONTENTS

Chapter **1**

Caring for the catch

After the joy of catching, the care begins.

Contents

CARING FOR THE CATCH

Your fish begins to spoil the minute you land it - this is no exaggeration! Enzymes and bacteria immediately go to work, taking away the wonderful, fresh flavors, and gradually making the fish unpalatable. Finally, these *spoilers* make your potentially tasty and nutritious catch, unusable. The time to start preventing these losses is *immediately* - as the commercial fisherman must do to keep his fish marketable.

Spoilers are in and on the fish

Enzymes are in the fish itself; they are natural parts of the life process while the fish lives. As soon as it stops living, however, they start to change the fresh flavors to stale - they even start to digest the fish itself. Next, the bacteria in the slime covering the fish, in its gills, and in its intestines rapidly multiply and help the enzymes with the *dirty work* of spoilage.

All the various preserving processes discussed in this book work by slowing the spoiling effects of enzymes and bacteria. Help these processes do a good job for you by reducing the numbers of *spoilers* as soon as possible. To get rid of the spoilers, BLEED, CLEAN, and COOL the fish as soon as you can.

1. Slime and scale the fish now if you can, it will only take another minute and it will never be easier than when the fish is freshest.

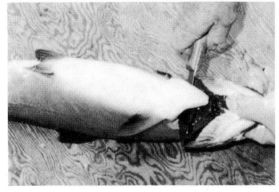

2. Immediate bleeding is best; the sooner you bleed the fish the better the blood removal. Getting rid of the blood not only removes spoiling enzymes, it also gives a more appetizing appearance. In pickled fish expecially, remaining blood turns dark and is repulsive looking.

3. Remove the gills; they are full of spoilage bacteria. Getting the blood and gills out is of immediate importance; the intestines can wait for several hours if the fish is kept cool. But it is *preferable* that they also come out *now* if you can manage it.

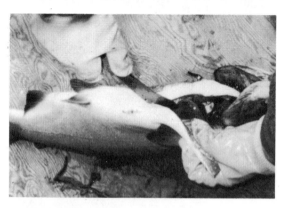

4. Remove the intestines; they are the source of millions of bacteria. Furthermore, the digestive enzymes of a feeding fish are so active they will continue their activity and begin to digest the fish itself.

5. Save the liver and roes; they are good fresh, but excellent smoked.

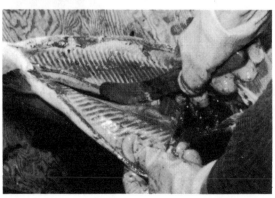

6. It is easier to remove the kidney, that dark streak along the backbone, if you carefully cut the covering membrane on either side of the kidney where it is attached to the flesh.

7. Scrape out the kidney thoroughly; it is the chief source of flavor destroying enzymes.

8. A well cleaned fish, kept cool, will ensure your later enjoyment. A good cleaning knife as shown here helps. This is a "Gut and Gill' knife used widely by Great Lakes commercial fishermen.

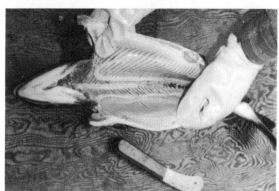

9. Removing the head now may be necessary to save cooler space; if so, you may want to leave the lug bone (that boney plate behind the head) on. If you later decide to smoke the fillet whole (see Smoking Whole Sides chapter 7), the lug bone will help support a handling cord.

10. Cool the fish. Now that you have removed most of the sources of spoilers, you *must* reduce the activity of those that are left. Both enzymes and bacteria spoil fish fastest at higher temperatures - 75 to 100° F (25 to 38° C) so get the temperature down, preferably close to freezing, as soon as you can. (See chapter 2 for details).

1. Careless landing and killing can damage fish. Gaffing, if used instead of a landing net, is best done in the least valuable part - the belly. But to even lose the belly in such economically valuable fish is a considerable waste.

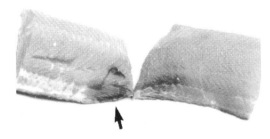

2. Kill the newly landed fish quickly to prevent its bruising itself by thrashing around. But do it carefully; aim to kill with one neat blow to the *head.*

I often witness fishermen go into a frenzy clubbing the fish all over its front end. Bruises such as these cause one or more servings to be lost.

~~~~~~~~~~~~~~~~~~~~~~~~~~~~~~

RIGOR MORTIS AND FISH QUALITY

There is another change beginning, as soon as fish are killed, that can also have an effect on fish quality. It is the stiffening, with which all fishermen are familiar, known as *rigor mortis.*

In life, as the fish swims and turns, its muscles are constantly contracting and relaxing. When the fish is killed, the muscles are at first relaxed while they use up stored energy. When the energy is gone, the muscles contract and stiffen (rigor mortis). After a time in *rigor,* the muscles again relax and stay that way.

How we can damage fish during rigor

If we physically disturb a fish in rigor by trying to straighten it out, or cause accelerated rigor by keeping the fish too warm, we damage it.

You can easily damage fish, which is much more fragile than meat, because fish muscle has very weak connective tissue. (Anyone who has cooked fish knows how fish flakes with just a little cooking). The flakes, or bundles of muscle, are held together by connective tissue, and more importantly, are also attached on one side to the skeleton, and on the other to the skin. If you forcibly straighten out a fish in rigor, or if the fish goes into heat-forced rigor, the muscle is literally *torn apart* by the strain.

When fish filets go into rigor above 65° F (18° C), they can temporarily *shrink* as much as 40% in length.

If you freeze them in this condition, they will often remain distorted when thawed later.

What rigor damage looks like

The effect of the muscle being torn is ragged looking fillets that are full of gaps, but the more important effect is that you lose the natural *juice* that gives the fish its succulence and flavor.

How to prevent rigor damage

Here again is where quickly cooling the fish is important. If you quickly get the fish cool, and keep it cool, it can pass through rigor normally. Then you'll have a good looking fish with the maximum of juiciness and flavor.

To get the best looking fillets, for smoking for instance, keep the whole (cleaned) fish cool until it has passed through rigor, then fillet it. Fresh fish for the making of smoked fillets, are routinely held on ice for at least three days by commercial producers, before filleting. If necessary, you can do a fairly decent job of filletting *before* rigor sets in, but don't expect a smooth, tasty fillet if you attempt it *during* rigor.

Your catch is valuable - care for it

I live very near a large fishing camp, so I often witness the care that sport fishermen give their catches; it ranges from fairly decent to plain awful. Please remember that your catch is a valuable piece of food, and needs the same care you would give a purchased piece of butcher's meat. Handle it always under the most sterile conditions possible, and keep it *cool.* If you take the time to check fish prices at the local supermarket, you will go away with a new respect for those finny ones that you may have been throwing in the bottom of your boat exposed to hot sun.

Chapter **2**

Cooling fish

On a hot summer day at some remote fishing spot, you've probably wished, as I have, for a refrigerator or freezer to cool your fish. Well, I've learned that even if such were possible, neither the freezer nor the frig would be the best tool for the cooling job. Further, I found that the perfect cooling device is usually readily available and is easy to carry into remote places - it is *plain old fashioned ice.*

Why is ice the perfect cooler

To cool fish, or anything, we must remove heat from it; something must absorb heat from the thing being cooled. Cooler air, or cooler water could absorb heat from the fish, but either would have to near freezing to cool the fish sufficiently. When the fish needs cooling the most, usually both the air and the water are as warm or warmer than it is.

Ice has a terrific ability to absorb heat *when it melts,* because when ice was made, an *extraordinary* amount of heat was removed from water to get it to freeze. The ice machine took heat from the water, and put it into the outside air. Now, when ice turns back into water, it absorbs that same *extraordinary* amount of heat it gave up when it was made. To illustrate this extraordinary capacity: 2 *pounds of ice* can do the same job of cooling fish as 37 *pounds of ice water.*

Ice is the best cooler for other reasons

Even if you could get a big home freezer to your remote fishing spot, it could only handle the same cooling load per hour as 9 lbs of *melting* ice. But the cold water from the melting ice, running over the fish, would to the job much faster than the cool air of the freezer. Water has many time the ability of air to carry heat away. Another advantage is that ice water would be washing millions of spoilage bacteria off the fish.

Please notice, above, that I said *melting* ice; that is the key to cooling with ice. For ice to cool, it must melt (change state from solid to liquid). When ice is melting on fish it is pulling heat out. If ice is insulated from the fish, it only cools the air that *may* pass between the two and under such circumstances there is very little cooling done.

How to get the fastest cooling from ice

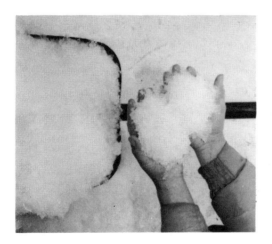

To get the fastest cooling, use *chipped* ice; finely enough chipped so that it will blanket the fish, wrap around it, touch it all over. Commercial fish handlers use a mush ice; it melts rapidly, and really cools the fish. *After* the fish is thoroughly cooled, *block* ice will usually do to handle the heat that comes through the walls of the fish container.

Ice needs to be all around the fish to be cooled, not just over, or under it, and the layer of fish must not be thick. If there are several layers of fish, without ice between them, the outside layers become excellent insulation that keeps the inside layer from cooling. For example: You can cool a 3 inch layer of fish from 60° F to 35° F in less than 3 hours. But, in a 6 inch layer of fish the center is still warm and getting stale 10 hours later.

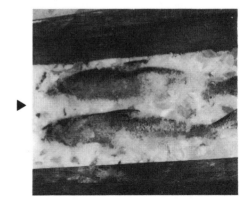

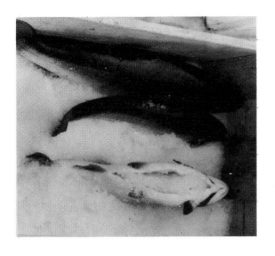

In getting ice all around the the fish for quick cooling, be careful about packing the belly cavity. Fat fish, such as chinook salmon, can stand to have the cavity packed with ice without worrying about the cavity draining. But other leaner trout and salmon must be iced so that the cavity can drain; pack the cavity but place the fish in a position (back up) that allows drainage.

ICE REQUIREMENTS

Cooling 15 lbs. (7kg) of fish to 33 °F (1 °C)

Fish Temperature	Ice Needed
65° F (19° C)	3½ lbs. (1.5 kg)
55° F)13° C)	2½ lbs. (1.2 kg)
45° F (7° C)	1½ lbs. (.75 kg)

The above amounts of ice are for cooling the fish only, and are based on the fish being in an insulated container. If the cooling container allows warm outside air access to the ice, more ice will be needed; at least twice the amounts shown.

Keeping 15 lbs. (7 kg) of COOL fish cool

Air Temperature	Ice Needed
100° F)38° C)	7 lbs. (3.25 kg)
90° F (32° C)	6 lbs. (2.75 kg)
80° F (27° C)	5 lbs. (2.00 kg)
70° F (20° C)	4 lbs. (1.75 kg)
60° F (15° C)	3 lbs. (1.50 kg)
50° F (10° C)	2 lbs. (1.00 kg)

The above amounts assume that a reasonably well insulated (foam or equal) container will be used. For uninsulated containers use twice to three times the amount shown. Be *sure* that the fish and ice are covered in any case.

The preceeding tables illustrate that if you have a well insulated cooler, you can *cool* 15 lbs. of fish from 60° F and *keep it cool* when it is 90° F outside, with 3 plus 6 for a total of 9 lbs. of ice.

Of course, the water from the chipped ice used for quick cooling, *must* be allowed to escape; the fish should *not* be allowed to stand in water at any time.

TRANSPORTING FROZEN FISH

If you are trying to keep *frozen* fish, however, ice will do no good. *Wet* ice at 32° F (0° C) will *thaw* frozen fish. To transport frozen fish, (which should be at 0° F. minus 20° C and then for a short time only), you need *dry* ice; its temperature is *minus* 109° F. You can see that it will further cool the already frozen fish.

I have carried frozen fish specimens around and across North America for several weeks in an insulated container. It takes planning to get from one dry ice supplier to another, but it can be done because the dry ice will last for two or three days.

Use the yellow pages to find sources of dry ice. It is often available at wet ice outlets, but the most dependable sources are the larger welding supply stores. Dry ice is a natural companion for their welding gas sales. One caution! Don't try to find dry ice on weekends or holidays. Remember! If you plan to move frozen fish, *plan ahead.* See also eutectic ice chapter 32.

Chapter **3**

The art of filleting

The processes we will be talking about: smoking, marinading, salting, freezing, and sausage making, require fillets in most cases. Canning is the major exception, because there the bones are cooked to edibility. Because filleting is important to the various processes, now before starting any of the processes, is the time to talk about it.

Filleting, the way the professional does it, is truly an art. Don't be intimidated by that fact, however, for if you will follow the illustrations and instruction given here, you will find it easier than you thought after doing a few fish.

1. Good tools are necessities for smooth, easy filleting. These include: either a bench (a), or a hand (b), stone; a steel for keeping the knife edge sharp between sessions with the stone (c); and the most important of all, a good filleting knife (d).

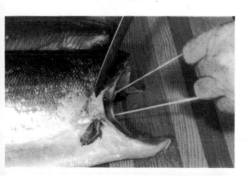

2. If you are removing the head now, in preparation for filleting, you may want to leave the lug bone on for easier handling (see REMOVING THE HEAD in chapter 1 this section).

3. Begin the filleting at the vent, making a cut on either side of the anal fin, just deep enough to reach the backbone. Make these cuts all the way to the tail.

4. Start the next cut on top of the backbone. You will immediately run into the belly bones which get tougher as the fish run bigger. Here is where the sharp knife comes in; it must be capable of cutting *through* the belly bones easily.

5. Continue the cut, working the knife along the backbone with the cutting edge slightly slanted toward the bone ...

6. ... all the way to the tail, and remove the first fillet. You can start the second cut either below the backbone or turn the fish over ...

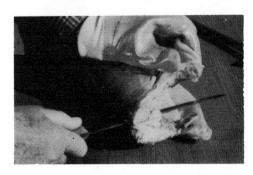

7. ... and make the second cut on top of the bone. Either way, keep the knife slightly slanted, and the pressure toward the bone.

8. Now you have two smooth fillets with little meat left on the backbone.

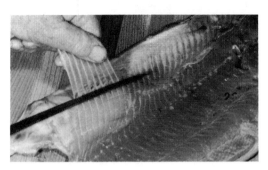

9. Now the belly bones can be removed easily without losing any edible meat.

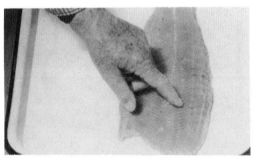

10. This leaves you with a boneless fillet except for the line of long, thin bones just above where the backbone used to be - you can feel their sharp ends with your finger.

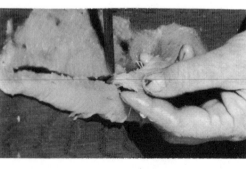

11. These last bones can be lifted out in a strip by making a cut on either side of the row of bones, just *to* the skin. Keep in mind, however that this deboning will spoil the fillet both in appearance and utility if you wish to make any of the smoked products that are thinly sliced.

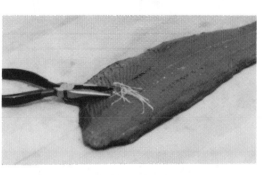

12. You can also do this final deboning, without marring the fillet, by pulling these bones with pliers. There are times, expecially with fresh fish, that these bones won't pull. In such cases, pull the bones after the fish is smoked.

Chapter **4**

Defatting
fat fish

Salmon and trout generally are fat fish, so you may have several reasons for wanting to defat them:

(1) To adhere to a fat restricted diet;

(2) To remove contaminants that may be in the fat of fish from certain waters. Health authorites of the Great Lakes region, in both the U.S. and Canada, warn against eating excessive amounts of certain fish because they may contain contaminants from mining, manufacturing and agriculture. The contaminants, if present, are concentrated in the fatty tissue. Authorities advise that the fatty tissue not be eaten - here's how you can remove much of it.

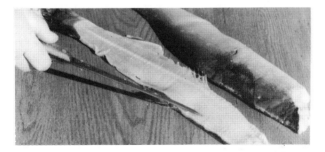

1. When you fillet, leave plenty of meat on the backbone where the meat is especially fat.

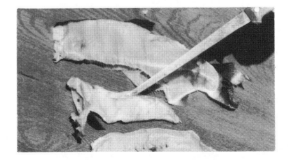

2. Completely cut off the belly portion; it is loaded with fat.

3. This amount of oil dripped from the belly flaps of a single, fat, lake trout during smoking.

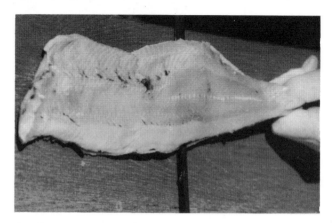

4. Skin the fillet, and leave about 1/8 inch (3mm) of meat on the skin.

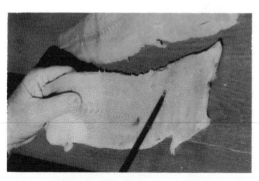

5. This layer, still attached to the skin, is very fatty.

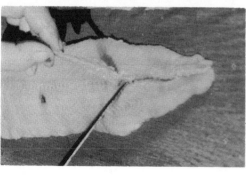

6. With the skin removed, you will find a streak of dark meat along the lateral line (middle of the fillet). Fat is concentrated in the dark meat; make a cut on either side of the streak, lift it out, and discard.

Chapter **5**

Boning
small trout

The most universally distributed member of the salmonids is the Rainbow Trout. From its start as a native of Western North America it has successfully been introduced, and become one of the favorite fishes of nearly every continent on the globe. Strangely, it's eating qualities are more respected in other parts of the world than they are in North America. I think that trout perhaps reach the peak of gastronomic appreciation in France. Possibly the reason for trout's appreciation comes from the effort that French Chefs put into their cooking and especially their boning in preparation for cooking. Here is how I borrow French methods to prepare smoked trout for special occasions (see chapter 13).

Of course there is nothing to prevent your using these boning methods and the special presentations for cooking *fresh* trout in the many recipes to be found in cookbooks, especially French cookbooks.

Smoking and serving the specially prepared smaller trout

Full instructions for smoking and serving these trout are given in the section on smoking, chapter 13.

Most smaller trout for smoking are simply cleaned and brined before smoking. Some Continental chefs, however, go to great lengths to prepare fish for special presentations.

Here are some special ways of preparing trout for smoking. Later when I talk about smoking trout, you will see how to handle these specially prepared trout in the smoker - followed by some ways of serving them.

BONING METHOD 1

In this method, you debone the fish through the back with the belly lef uncut. Obviously this can only be done with fish that have not been cleanec in the usual way (through the belly). The fish, therefore, must really be fresh.

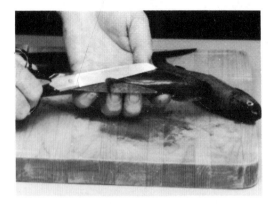

1. Snip the fins off all the way around.

2. Cut the gills loose at the throat.

3. Grasp the gills and pull them loose . . .

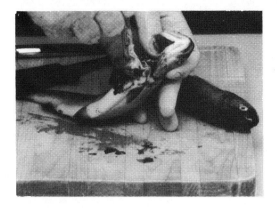

4. ... along with most of the intestines.

5. Now carefully make a cut on one side of the back-bone ...

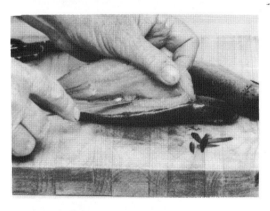

6. ... working the meat loose along the backbone, and all the way to the belly. Be careful not to cut through the belly skin.

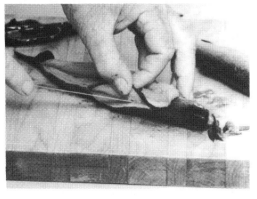

7. Repeat the operation on the other side.

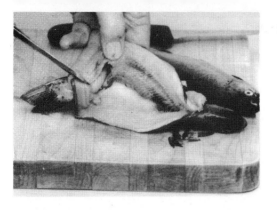

8. Now snip the backbone off as close to the tail as possible ...

9. ... then at the head.

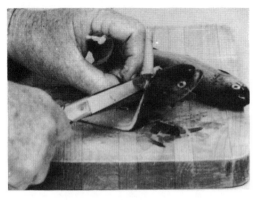

10. Now you can finish cleaning the belly cavity.

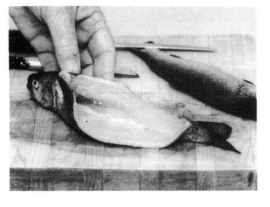

11. There you have a deboned fish that can be smoked and used in a special luncheon presentation.

BONING METHOD 2

In this method normally cleaned fish are boned through the belly. The back skin is left uncut.

1. Make a cut from the vent, along either side of the back-bone to the tail.

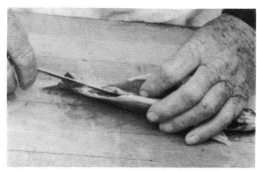

2. Then carefully work the meat loose from the ribcage ...

3. ... and along the backbone down to, but *not* through the skin of the back.

4. Then snip off the backbone close to the tail.

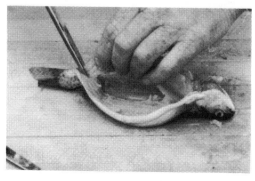

5. Pull the bone free up to the head ...

6. ... then snip it off.

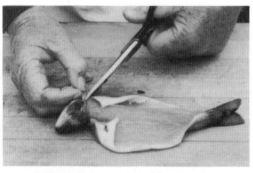

7. trim off the fins.

8. Now pull the tail out through the mouth.

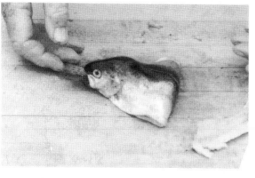

9. The fish is ready for smoking for a special presentation.

BONING METHOD 3

In this method fish that have been cleaned through the belly, are boned through the back; thus both the belly and the back are open at the finish.

1. Cut along both sides of the backbone.

2. Carefully work the meat loose over both sides of the ribcage.

3. Snip the bone off at the tail ...

4. ... then at the head.

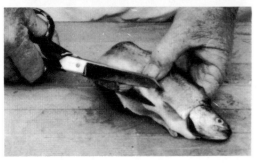

5. Trim the fins off.

6. Now the boneless fish is ready for smoking.

7. Or the tail may be cut off ...

8. ... and the sides rolled, skin out ...

9. ... for smoking and serving in a special presentation.

2
SMOKING

CONTENTS

Chapter **6**

About smoking

Smoked Salmon! That phrase stirs up pleasant gustatory sensations in most people. It says, "Gourmet delight!" "Lavish entertaining!" "Exotic, expensive, taste treat!" But what is this food that brings such visions of opulence? How would you describe it? Description is difficult because it means *many quite different* things to different people.

To inhabitants of Ireland and the British Isles, and to gourmets around the world, *smoked salmon* is cold smoked salmon or trout that has a texture like cured ham, and is thinly sliced to be eaten raw. It can also be a similar product from Scandinavia, or Nova Scotia.

To native people of western Canada, and those of some Scandinavian countries, *smoked salmon* means a salmon, char, or trout that has been dried and smoked until it will keep without further preservation.

To inhabitants of the west coast of the U.S. and Canada, *smoked salmon* is salmon that is chunked, dyed red, then *hot smoked*.

To delicatessen patrons of North America, *smoked salmon* probably means *lox*, which may mean most anything. The fish may *not even have been smoked* - it may only have been sugar and salt cured.

To the millions of sportsmen and others who own aluminum box - and - hotplate smokers, *smoked salmon* is their own *smoke cooked* product, and so the list of these succulent treats goes on and on. All of the traditional *smoked salmon* - like products, fortunately for those who don't live in salmon country, can be made from any of the larger trout or landlocked salmon as well as true salmon.

I know there will be those that find it hard to accept the idea of making Lox from Lake trout, or Scotch Smoked Salmon, from steelhead, but why not? The most famous of the smoked salmons is Scotch Smoked Atlantic salmon. But the Atlantic is not a true salmon; it is a *trout*. And now that there aren't enough Atlantic Salmon to fill the demand for Scotch Smoked Salmon, Pacific Cohos and Chinooks are imported for this purpose. Probably 99 percent of the consumers can't tell the difference.

I have successfully made all the traditional smoked salmons from a wide variety of salmon, trout, and chars - so can you - that's what this section is all about.

Now that I have proven to myself that traditional smoked salmon products can be as successfully made from other salmonids (trout & chars), I'll simply call all the products *salmon* and you use which ever species is available to you.

Good Smoking!

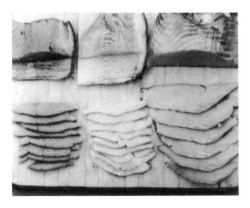 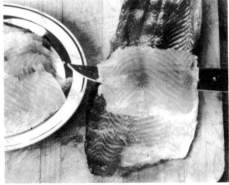

Scotch Smoked Pacific salmon, Lake Trout, and Great Lakes Coho

Scotch Smoked Rainbow Trout

ABOUT ALL THE KINDS OF SMOKED SALMON

Did you notice in the above discussion that some of the smoked salmon were cold smoked and others hot smoked? Why the difference? It's mostly a matter of personal taste; connoisseurs want their salmon to have a texture like cured ham. They want to be able to slice it thin and eat it raw, because to them that is smoked salmon at its uniquely flavorful best. Other smoked salmon lovers wouldn't get caught dead eating raw fish; they want it cooked - hot smoked.

The difference between the two products is not subtle. Both hot and cold smoked can be delicious, but they are as different as night and day; as different as fish and meat.

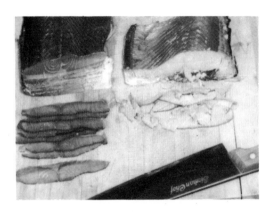

Hot and cold smoked pieces from the same fish. Note how the cold smoked on the left has retained or intensified the natural color and slices thinly without crumbling. The hot smoked color has faded, and it crumbles when sliced.

Kinds of smoked salmon

HOT SMOKED	Barbecued Kippered Canned smoked Smoked small trout
COLD SMOKED	Scotch - Irish - Norweigen - Nova Scotia Lox Indian or hard smoked Pickled smoked Selachs Roes and livers

Some of the many kinds of smoked fish during testing to find best smoking conditions

About barbecued salmon

Barbecued or smoke-cooked salmon is what you get when you use a covered barbecue or one of the box-and-hotplate smokers. These units are designed for smoke *cooking* only, and usually you have no control over temperature. My definition of barbecued salmon is: cooking in a smokey atmosphere without any preliminary cold smoking or low temperature conditioning.

About kippered salmon

Kippered salmon is different from barbecued because you condition it to heat *gradually* before hot smoking it. By contrast, in *barbecueing*, you put the fish into a *preheated* oven and leave it there until it is cooked. In kippering, you first dry the fish in barely warm air, then *gradually* bring it up to hot smoking temperature to improve its appearance and quality. Usually, if fish is heated too rapidly, juice that contains soluble protein, comes to the surface. There it forms puddles and then dries into unsightly white curds. Too rapid heating also often causes the surface to crack and dry unevenly.

Originally the name kipper was given to Atlantic salmon caught in the European rivers as they returned to the sea after spawning. The spent fish were so emaciated, that they were smoked to give them a more attractive color and general appearance. The Dutch gave these fish the name Kuppen, which means to spawn.

Later, smoked herring were also given the name kipper, presumably because they too were smoked. It became the custom later to dye kippered herring to give a *smoked* color with less smoking time.

Later still, when smoked Pacific salmon became popular, the white chinooks couldn't be sold alongside the red variety unless they were *dyed* red. Soon the dyed salmon, or any dyed fish was called *kippered*. The dying adds nothing but color, and to me is ridiculous because the product looks phoney as soon as the surface is broken and the different undercolor shows.

About smoked salmon for canning

Smoked salmon for canning must be specially prepared; it isn't just smoked salmon that you later decide to can. The rigorous pressure cooking that is necessary to sterilize canned fish can do a number of undesirable things to it. It can make the pellicle much too dark, it can concentrate the smoke flavor and it can release moisture that makes the product soupy.

To prevent these undesirable side effects, you must give the fish special handling. First to prevent pellicle darkening, put the fish directly into a preheated smoker. This brings oil to the surface, and minimizes pellicle formation; the darkening thus is reduced. Secondly, reduce the amount of smoking that the fish gets so that when the smaller amount of smoke is concentrated, it ends up tasting just right. Lastly, dry the fish more, in the smoker, than you would other smoked products. Commercial canners nearly always dry fish before canning; this is how such fish as canned sardines become smoked in the first place. The first primitive canned sardines were too soupy, so they were dried over fires - the smoking was incidental or accidental.

About smoked small trout

These are a real delicacy, seldom found on North American menus. They are offered, along with smoked salmon, by many eating places in the British Isles and Europe. Usually eaten as appetizers, they are eaten cold.

For appetizers, trout over 9 inches (23 cm) long are too big. For serving at lunch or cold supper, smoke fish up to 12 inches (30 cm). I find it unhandy to smoke any bigger trout whole.

There may be another important reason to smoke trout: Smoking takes away the *muddy* or *mossy* taste they sometimes have, caused by otherwise harmless molds, algae, etc. in the fish's environment. Fortunately we have a threshold for flavors and odors, and another flavor or odor, like smoke, can cover the undesirable one.

About Scotch smoked salmon

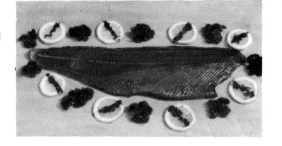

Gourmets appreciate this product more than any other smoked salmon. You may eat it under different names: Irish, Scandinavian, or Nova Scotia, but they are essentially made the same way.

Scotch smokers originally used Atlantic salmon; since today's demand for this specie cannot be met, the Pacific Coho, and to a lesser extent the chinook, are used to supplement the supply of Atlantic salmon.

Anyone not familiar with the Scotch smoked product might wonder why it brings much higher prices than hot smoked salmon. Probably for the same reason that New York steak is more expensive than ground beef from the same steer. If nicely broiled, the ground beef often has a better flavor than the steak. But then we pay two to three times as much for the steak, because of the steak's succulence and texture; it has *bite appeal*. Perhaps that is how people feel about Scotch smoked salmon.

Scotch type, cold smoked salmon is a difficult product to make. The smoker must acquire some skill in salting and be able to *feel* when the right texture has been reached in the smoking. Because more care is required, I do this kind of smoking only when I want to serve the fish raw, or wish to have slices of smoked salmon to use in a special cooked dish - a special display. For the many hot dishes we prepare at home, we use kippered salmon which is easier to process.

About lox

The word LOX has become a very confusing term. Originally it was used to designate smoked salmon made from mild-salted fish, and originally it was not lox, but lachs - the German word for salmon. Germans had long smoked the Atlantic salmon caught in the rivers around the North Sea. When the salmon supply dwindled, enterprising German fish merchants went looking to America where an infant Pacific salmon salting industry had begun. The *hard salted* salmon being produced weren't suitable for the German taste, so the American salters were persuaded to put up a *mild cure*.

This mild cured fish, when desalted and smoked, became very popular in sandwiches in the German beerhalls.

European immigrants in America soon demanded the same product, and here it became *lox*. This mild-cured, smoked salmon became extremely popular, especially in centers with large Jewish populations. Lox producers did, and still do, pay a premium for larger salmon that will provide the best lox. Fisherman call these premium fish *Smilies;* that's what they bring at the payoff.

There are still some salmon being mild salted for lox, but this is an expensive means of preservation. Because of the small amount of salt used, the barrels of fish must be stored under refrigeration. The barrels take a lot of cooler space, and must be constantly overhauled because of evaporation. For this reason, and because changing tastes wanted a less salty, less *cured* product, lox processors have in recent years quit using the mild-cured fish. Now that there is a dependable supply of frozen salmon, lox makers thaw them, briefly salt-sugar cure them, and then smoke slightly. This modern version of lox is known to some of the trade as *Nova Lox*. It doesn't have the same flavor as the older, cured product, but that makes it popular for modern tastes.

Today, what the delicatessens may still call *smoked salmon*, isn't. Many lox makers simply salt and sugar salmon, sometimes with the addition of spices - no smoking! Now lox is often called *Lox Salmon* instead of smoked salmon.

About hard smoked

or indian smoked salmon

Many of us would like to make a jerky-like product from the salmon and trout we catch. This is what *hard smoked* salmon is; it is so dried that it will keep without freezing or other preservation. You can use such a dried product for snacking, for an emergency or trail food, or to add a unique flavor to stews, soups and other dishes.

Although our native Indians originated this hard smoked preservation of salmon, the name *hard smoked* was attached to a similar product when early commercial fishermen, who at that time used only salting for keeping fish, found they could *cash in* on the repeal of *prohibition*. With the opening of taverns and bars, there came the need for snacks that would encourage thirst, and yet keep well while on display. Why not desalt the salted salmon and smoke-dry it like the Indians did, they thought. The resulting fish was surely hard smoked - all of the directions for making the product call for smoking for two weeks or more! That's too smoky for me, as has been most of the hard smoked salmon I've tasted. I've found, however, that if I take a tip from the Indians, hard smoked salmon needn't be too smoky.

The early Indians, inhabitants of the salmon country, found their food situation to be either feast or famine. In the late summer and fall, salmon were so plentiful that they literally choked the streams. Then followed the long, fishless, hungry winter. To avoid famine, those early fishermen had to keep some of the fish from the time of plenty for the time of want. One of the easiest ways for these native fishermen to keep fish was to dry it. If a wind blew in salmon season, it made drying easy, but the weather then, as now, was undependable in salmon country. More often than not, drying by *fire* was necessary and that meant the drying fish also got smoked. To help the drying process the Indians cut the salmon fillets into *strips*, and by adopting this idea I can get drying in hours instead of weeks and have a product that will keep well without being too smoky. For example, if I cut the fish into strips, and expose more of the surface to the drying air of my forced-draft smoker, it will dry well in 30 hours. If I have the smoke on only part of that time, I get just the right flavor.

About pickled smoked salmon

We aren't always fortunate enough to catch fish at peak quality for eating. Often, in early spring, fish aren't fat, and therefore are bland tasting. In the fall they may be too fat and equally uninteresting to eat. Often smoking such fish will make them much more appetizing, but sometimes you may want to make them even more interesting by adding additional flavor. Here is the answer: pickle-smoke them.

Canadian Fisheries researchers put a good pickle cure together in an effort to make the Pacific Chum salmon more useful commercially. The Chum, because it contains less flavoring fat than other salmon, does not have their rich taste because the Chum lacks flavor, and because it loses all color when cooked, it isn't well accepted by discriminating consumers. This pickle-smoke process transforms it into something special. It also works well for the other salmonids; I have used it on the overly fat Lake Trout from Lake Ontario, and also on the almost fat-free, early spring trout with equally gratifying results.

About seelachs
the ersatz smoked salmon

Exotic smoked delicacies from salmon, trout and chars; this has been my theme. I have talked about making these usually expensive, gourmet products from the trout and salmon we catch or buy. "But" say many, "None of these are available to me, so forget it." Don't give up! Let me tell you what other smoked salmon lovers did under such circumstances - they make an ersatz (fake) smoked salmon.

When the salmon loving Germans had their salmon supply cut-off during World War 1, they were not satisfied to do without altogether. Enterprizing German fish merchants learned to take ordinary white fish from the ocean, and make them into a salmon substitute. This became known as *Seelachs - ocean* salmon.

Seelachs are even dyed to look like salmon. If you have ever bought any kippered salmon or kippered Alaska cod, you know how difficult it is to dye fish. Remember how the dye is only on the surface? One can only get a *minor* penetration of the dye in a reasonable time. Well, the seelachs merchants solve this problem by slicing the fish into thin enough slices so the dye penetrates all the way through. They first treat the fish with salt long enough to firm it for good slicing, dye it with harmless food coloring, then smoke it lightly. The finished product looks like nice, rich, smoked salmon, expecially if you don't have any salmon around to compare it with.

Smoked roes and livers

The obvious use of salmon and trout roes is in red caviar, the making of which is fully described in chapter 26. But for those who have an aversion to raw fish eggs, the roes - both *hard* (female) and *soft* (male) - become a delectable food when smoked. This is also true of the livers which are milder than many animal or fowl livers.

The smoked roes have a number of uses; they may be simply fried, cooked with eggs, used in spreads and dips, in sauces and casseroles, or combined with the smoked livers to make delicious pates.

Chapter **7**

The smoking process

What happens when you smoke fish? Most importantly you get a smoke *flavor*, next in importance is the drying that occurs. The drying is important because it contributes more than the smoking to the keeping quality of the fish. Drying also improves the texture of the fish - makes it more appealing to eat.

In the hot smoking process, you also *cook* the fish while smoking it.

Well defined steps help you accomplish these things. By following these steps each time you smoke, you will ensure predictable results.

Steps in the smoking process

Filleting
Cutting
Salting
Curing
Smoking
Final Preservation

Filleting

Filleting is important because it exposes the fish flesh to the salt and smoke, and allows faster drying. (see chapter 3). If you smoke fish in the round (whole) it takes an unreasonably and unpredictably long time to get salt and then smoke into the flesh.

Small trout are the only fish I suggest smoking in the round, but even they benefit by having the skin *slit* to allow penetration.

Smoking whole fillets vs. pieces

In a fine dining place we may see a whole side of Scotch smoked salmon exhibited in solitary splendor as a symbol of their excellent cuisine. Likewise, we may occasionally want to display a full side of smoked salmon for some gala affair in our own homes. For these rare occasions it may well be worth your time and trouble to smoke a whole side, but for ordinary use it will be easier and more economical to salt and smoke the easy way - cutting the sides into pieces as illustrated.

Sides of fish salt and smoke better if they are cut into pieces according to thickness. Pieces can then be salted, smoked, and dried for different lengths of time; there is no need to over or under treat any portion in order to get the greater part right. If your smoker isn't set to handle pieces, *change it*. Make up racks for holding the pieces or tenter sticks for hanging them - you will be much happier with results.

Other reasons for smoking the sides or fillets in pieces are: (1) You can use the thicker pieces for products like lox, or Scotch smoked that are to be thin sliced. Then the thinner pieces can be hot smoked, canned, or Indian smoked. (2) If you smoke the fish in pieces, the attractive covering (pellicle) forms all over the piece. You get not only a more attractive, finished-looking product, but also a better protected product for freezing. Smoked fatty fish tend to go rancid from oxidization after a few months in the freezer. When you process *pieces* the smoke deposits antioxidants all over the pieces and protects them better from rancidity. If you smoke a whole side, then cut it into pieces, obviously the cut ends are unprotected and open to rancidity.

Salting before smoking

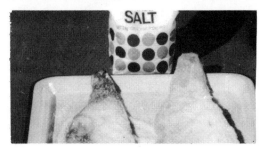

Salting does several necessary things:
It flavors the fish.
It releases moisture from the flesh, thus helping dry the fish
It modifies the fish flesh - firms it as much or as little as you wish. *Moderate* salting can change the fish *texture* ever so slightly to improve its eating quality. *Prolonged* salting can *harden* raw fish so you can then slice it for serving.

What kind of salt?

There is only one salt to use - PURE. For the home smoker *pickling salt* is the purest salt normally available. Ignore recipies that call for rock salt of unknown purity, and don't use table salt with its additives - use only pure *pickling* salt.

Curing after salting

Curing is an expression I have added to the smoking process. Smoking technologists simply refer to draining the fish after salting, but there is more happening during this time than getting rid of surplus brine. Some famous Scotch and Irish salmon smokers *drain* the fish for as long as 24 hours before smoking. During this time the fish is drying somewhat, and the salt is equilibrating - evening-out - throughout the fish. But I detect another important process going on at the same time - *flavor is developing*.

When I was observing Scotch and Irish salmon smokers, I noted that this *curing* between salting and smoking was a carefully followed ritual.

Smoking

We have already discussed the fact that some of the smoking processes are hot and others cold. You can use nearly any sort of a device to smoke cook fish, but if you wish to perform some of the cold smoking processes, the smoker must be more sophisticated.

Fish smokers can, and do, come in every conceivable size and shape. They vary from simple boxes with a hotplate, through revamped refrigerators, to complicated commercial devices with six figure price tags.

Most commercial smokers have abandoned the old fashioned *natural* draft smoker because of its undependability. The *natural* draft smoker depends on being able to heat the air to create a draft. If the weather is warm, it is impossible to heat the air further and still be able to cold smoke (85° F maximum).

Modern smokers are *forced* draft and *air conditioned,* and can be dependably used in any weather. With control over all conditions, smoking results are predictably the same each time rather than full of surprises as they are in old fashioned smokers.

I have designed and built a small, air conditioned, forced draft smoker, and have thoroughly enjoyed its use for more than 5 years. I'm sure that many other home smokers have built similar units.

Forced draft smokers require much less smoking time than traditional natural draft smokers, Accordingly, I have instructions for the two kinds.

For a more comprehensive look at smokers, smoking accessories, and smoking fuels, see chapter 18.

Preserving after smoking

Final preservation after smoking is important, because smoked fish, with the exception of Indian smoked, keeps very little better than fresh. Today we smoke fish for flavor, and we want the flavor mild. We also don't want the fish too dry, or too salty. As a result it is quite perishable, and we must refrigerate, freeze, or can it promptly.

Mild smoked fish, like Scotch smoked, has a limited shelf life in the refrigerator - about two to three weeks. If you let it sit in the frig for a week before deciding to freeze the surplus, one third of its shelf life will be gone when you later thaw it.

The following chapters give detailed instructions for making all the different kinds of smoked salmon and trout delicacies that have been discussed.

Chapter **8**

Scotch smoking

Please read about Scotch Smoking in chapter 6.

Since this product is more widely known and is considered to be *The Smoked Salmon* by many, I chose to talk about making it, first. It is the most difficult smoking process, so the description is necessarily more complex and complete than others.

You have seen earlier that Scotch Smoking can be done with fish prepared in either of these 2 ways:

      1. A full side

      2. Pieces cut according to thickness

For reasons that I will give in a moment, each way calls for a different method of *salting*.

THE SMOKING PROCESS

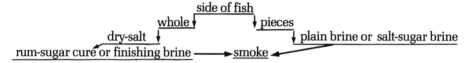

Don't *brine-salt a whole side*, the *thinner parts* - tail and belly - get far too much salt while the *thick parts* are getting enough; attempts to compromise between the two spoil the final product. Dry-salt!

Dry salting allows you to place a specific amount of salt on each part of the side according to thickness. If you allow the brine, that results from the moisture being drawn from the fish, to run off (away from the thin parts), saltiness of the various parts can be controlled. With *pieces cut according to thickness*, on the other hand, you can easily *brine-salt* for the required time, according to *thickness*.

Salt alone or with sugar, etc.?

For dry-salting Scotch Smoked, use plain pickling salt, not a mixture. If you want some flavors other than salt, I have described a special Scotch Cure that comes *after* the dry-salting. It is necessary to use *only* salt in the beginning to *condition* the flesh so that you can eventually slice it *thin* for serving. Once you have conditioned the flesh, *then* other flavors can be introduced. (see Rum - Sugar Cure for Scotch Smoking).

If you don't wish to introduce other flavors after dry-salting, take away some salt-caused hardness by using a short brine treatment (see Finishing Brine).

Brine-salting of pieces is another matter. Unlike dry salting, sugar and spices can be added to the salt in making the brine if you wish. Or, you can simply use a plain salt brine.

Be cautious about using added flavors to salt before Scotch smoking, however, because the combination of prime salmon, salt, and cold smoke is hard to beat. That combination gives the subtle flavor that keeps epicures coming back for more.

Adding flavors to the salt, under certain conditions. is sometimes waranted, however. You may want to:

a. Give flavor to an otherwise bland fish - one too thin or too fat.

b. Cover-up a muddy, or mossy flavor.

c. Satisfy your own individual taste.

d. Soften the taste of salt.

Sequence of instruction for Scotch smoking

I. Salting Process:	a. Dry-salting whole sides	1. Plain salt or
		2. Salt then sugar, rum
	or	
	b. Brine-salting pieces	1. Plain salt or
		2. Salt, sugar, spice
II. Smoking Process:	Done after a1 or a2	or b1 or b2.

DRY-SALTING WHOLE SIDES FOR SCOTCH SMOKING

Dry-salting sequence

1. Cut thick sides lengthwise into 2 fillets or inject brine into thick portion.

2. Cut through skin and rub salt in.

3. Apply salt.

Thick fish a special problem

Thick sides (2 in. or thicker) are hard to get dry-salted through. You can either cut the side lengthwise into two thinner fillets or inject a salt brine into the thick portion. For injecting, you will need a pumping needle (*see page 230).

Injection brine

Make up enough 90° salinometer brine so you can inject 1 to 1½ oz. (30 to 45 ml) per pound of fish - 65 to 100 ml per Kilo of fish.

90° sal. brine

Pickling salt	Water
10 oz. (1¼ cup)	1 qt.
or	
300 g (300 ml)	1 l

Cool the injection brine to at least 60°F (15°C) before using it. Inject into the thick part before applying the dry-salt. Be sure that any excess brine can drain away *from* the thin parts, because if they stand in brine (also brine from disolving dry-salt) they will be too salty. You may as well have brined the whole side in the first place. To accomplish the draining, arrange all the thin parts in the same direction so that by tilting the tray the brine will drain away from them.

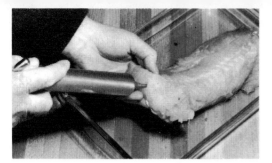

Inject brine into thick sides

To get better penetration of salt, score the skin as shown

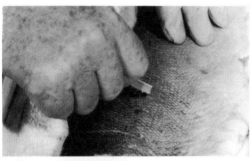

Use a razor blade or very sharp knife to cut *just* through the skin into the fatty layers below

Rub salt into the cuts then lay the side, skin side down on a ¼ in (6 mm) layer of salt

Place salt on the side according to thickness - up to a ½ in. on the thickest part and less on the thinner parts, down to just a sprinkling near the tail.

Dry-salting times

Dry-salting time depends on how thick and how fat the fish is. It obviously takes longer for salt to get through a thicker fish. Fatness controls salt penetration this way: A fish's body is made up of water, protein and fat. The only way *dry-salt* can get into a fish is to disolve in the body water. If a fish is fat, it contains proportionately less water, therefore it dissolves and absorbs salt more slowly.

Drysalting times for Scotch smoked whole sides

Fillet Thickness	Fat Fish	Lean Fish
¾ in.	9 hrs.	5 hrs.
1 in.	12 hrs.	7 hrs.
1¼ in.	15 hrs.	8½ hrs.
1½ in.	18 hrs.	10 hrs.
2 in.	24 hrs.	13 hrs.
2½ in.	30 hrs.	17 hrs.
3 in.	36 hrs.	20 hrs.

Telling when Scotch salmon is dry-salted enough

You will learn to feel when your Scotch salmon is salted enough. The table I have given is only useful in getting a start. A fair guide to telling when the side is salted enough is weight loss; a moderately fat fish will lose about 10% of its weight during salting. The best way for you to tell about salting is by feel. When you press the fillet, either with the forefinger or between the thumb and forefinger, it will feel firm and spring back if salted enough. If the surface feels firm, but underneath it still feels soft, give the side more time in the salt.

Keep a record of how must salt you placed and how long you left it on. Also record the thickness of the fish and try to estimate its fatness. Next time you can either duplicate a successful process or improve an inferior one.

AFTER DRY-SALTING

You have a choice of doing one of two things before smoking: 1. Continue on with a special Scotch sugar-rum cure or 2. Use a finishing brine.

SPECIAL SCOTCH SUGAR-RUM CURE

1. After the side has been rinsed of the dry-salt, drain (cure) it in a cool place for 6 hours

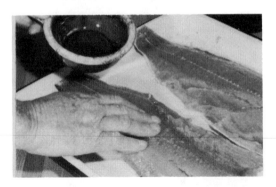

2. Rub it with vegetable oil (olive or peanut are favorites) and let it stand for 6 hours in a cool place

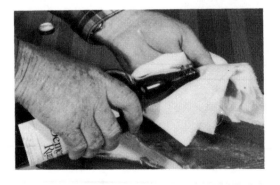

3. Rub off the oil with a rum soaked cloth

4. Cover the side with brown sugar just as you did with dry-salt, and let it stand in a cool place for 6 hours.

5. After the sugar treatment, wipe off the sugar, again coat with oil and let stand for six hours.

6. Wipe off the oil again with a rum soaked cloth, and the salmon is ready to smoke.

Turn now to the smoking instructions.

If not using the special Scotch cure

If you have chosen not to use the sugar-rum cure, use a finishing brine to take away some of the hardness caused by the dry-salt. It will also distribute the salt through the flesh.

30° sal. finishing brine

Pickling Salt	Water
11 oz. wt. or liq.	4 qt.

or

| 340 g or ml | 4 l |

Leave the side in the brine according to thickness: 20 min. for ¾ in. thick to 90 min. for 2 in. thick.

Once out of the finishing brine, the hardness should be gone from the fish. When you press the side, it should feel like the lean part of slab bacon.

Draining after brining

After removing fish from the finishing brine, drain it skinside down. Make sure that no brine collects on the surface where it will dry into unsightly salt deposits.

While the fish is draining a salt gloss is forming and the fish is curing. Allow overnight or about 12 hours for this draining process, but keep the fish at a temperature *no higher* than 70° F (20° C).

If you find you would like a more cured flavor in your finished product, increase the above draining curing time.

Turn to Smoking Instructions.

Resume: Dry-salting *whole sides* for Scotch smoking.

a. Cut skin for better salt penetration and rub salt into the cuts.
b. Apply salt to fish according to thickness of the flesh. Inject brine into thicker fish.
c. Learn to feel when fish is salted enough.
d. Choose to follow dry-salting with either a sugar-rum cure or a finishing brine.
e. Drain and cure fish before smoking.

BRINING PIECES FOR SCOTCH SMOKING

Choose a brine, either *plain* salt or *salt-mix* (salt-sugar-spices).

Plain salt brine

for Scotch smoking pieces.

90° sal. brine

Pickling Salt	Water
20 oz. (2½ cups)	64 oz.

or

630 g (630 ml)	2 l

Cool the brine before using and keep it cool while in use. If you can't keep the fish and brine in a cool place below 50° F (10° C), put ice in a *watertight* container in the brine. Don't add ice directly to the brine. It will melt and delute the brine, throwing your brining time off.

About brining times

The table below includes only the thicker pieces that make suitable slices when smoked. The thinner pieces I use in other ways.

Brining Times (Plain salt)

Piece Thickness	Fat Fish	Lean Fish
¾ in.	2 hrs.	1 1/3 hrs.
1 in.	3 hrs.	2 hrs.
1¼ in.	4 hrs.	2 2/3 hrs.
1½ in.	5 hrs.	3 1/3 hrs.
1¾ in.	6 hrs.	4 hrs.
2 in.	8 hrs.	5 1/3 hrs.
*2½ in.	10 hrs.	6 2/3 hrs.
*3 in.	12 hrs.	8 hrs.

*These thicker pieces will benefit by having brine pumped into the thickest part with a meat pumping needle as discussed under dry-salting.

Salt-mix (salt-sugar-spice) brine
for Scotch smoking pieces

Pickling Salt	Sugar (white or brown)	Water
36 oz. (4½ cups)	12 oz. (1½ cups)	128 oz.
	or	
1120 g (1120 ml)	370 g (370 ml)	4 l

Add spices, if you wish. Choose from the following: adjust the amount to suit your taste:

Bayleaf (50 leaves, crushed	Mace 2 tbs. or 30 ml
Pepper 8 tsp. or 40ml	Juniper Berries 5 tbs. or 30 ml (crushed)

Simmer spices in brine for 45 min. Then strain brine through a cloth lined strainer or funnel. Discard spices and cool the brine.

Brining times (salt-mix)

Piece Thickness	Fat Fish	Lean Fish
¾ in.	2½ hrs.	1½ hrs.
1 in.	3½ hrs.	2½ hrs.
1¼ in.	4¾ hrs.	3¼ hrs.
1½ in.	6 hrs.	4 hrs.
1¾ in.	7¼ hrs.	4¾ hrs.
2 in.	9½ hrs.	6½ hrs.
2½ in.	12 hrs.	8 hrs.
3 in.	14¼ hrs.	9½ hrs.

Telling when fish is brined enough

The brining times are intended as a guide, because each fish may be different. You will learn to tell when the fish is salted enough by feel. It will be firm enough for slicing when it feels like the lean part of slab bacon when pressed between thumb and forefinger, after the fish pieces come out of the brine.

You will learn to tell when the fish is salted enough by feel.

After brining, place the fish pieces skin side down so they can drain. If the fish is drained on the smoking trays, tilt the trays so that no brine collects on the surface. If brine collects, it will form unsightly salt deposits when it dries.

Time for draining and curing:

While the fish is draining, a salt gloss is forming and the fish is curing. Drain the fish overnight (about 12 hours) at a temperature not higher than 70°F (20°C).

Resume: Brining *Pieces* for Scotch Smoking

a. Choose and make either a plain salt or a salt-sugar-spice brine.
b. Cool the brine and keep it cool.
c. Brine fish according to thickness and fattness.
d. Learn to *feel* when fish is brined enough.
e. Drain and cure fish before smoking.

HOW TO SCOTCH SMOKE

The properly salted and drained salmon now needs smoke color and flavor and sufficient drying for good slicing and texture.

Often there is sufficient color and flavor *before* the fish is dried enough for good texture. In such cases the fish needs more drying at the same temperature - 85°F (30°C) *without* further smoking. Too much smoke, especially from tarry woods like alder can ruin the fish.

In smokers with supplementary heat, drying can continue with the smoke off. In smokers without supplementary heat, a small, clear fire with as little smoke as possible is necessary to continue the drying process.

One caution about using smoke color as a guide to amount of smoke: The color acquired in a given smoking time is dependent on the smoking *temperature*. For example you will get much greater color development at a smoking temperature of 85°F (30°C) than you will at 50°F (10°C). You may be depositing the same amount of smoke at the lower temperature but not getting the color development. If one time you smoke at 85° F and get a desirable color and flavor, then next time smoke at 50°F until you get the same color, you will get too much smoke flavor.

Smoking sequence

a. Smoke for sufficient color.
b. Dry further without smoke if more firming needed.
c. Give the fish a *polished* look.
d. Sweat fish for further firming.
e. Refrigerate for further firming.

Scotch Smoking Process

Smoke time, temperature, and density for both forced and natural draft smokers (see chapter 9).

Smoking

Forced-Draft Smoker	Natural-Draft Smoker
Smoke Temp. 85° F (30° C)	85° F (30° C)
Smoke Time 10 to 12 hours	Up to 24 hours
	depending on weather
Smoke Density medium	light to medium

Continue drying if the fish isn't firm enough for slicing.

Drying

	Forced Draft	Natural Draft
Smoke	None	As little as possible
Temp.	85° F (30°C)	85° F (30° C)
Time	1 to 3 hours	Up to 24 hours

Give a polish to the fish with a moderate *burst* of heat (100°F - 38°C) for 15 minutes. This will bring a bit of oil to the surface.

Weight loss from salting and smoking for fat fish, will be around 18%; for thinner fish up to 25%.

For fish not firm enough still, resort to what is known in the smoking trade as *sweating*. Let the fish stand in a cool place until moisture comes to the surface (up to 24 hours or more). Then continue drying in the smoker.

Improved slicing in difficult fish will come from letting the fish condition in the refrigerator for a few days.

Cool the fish before wrapping. Even though it may only be 85°F, it will sweat if wrapped before cooling and quickly spoil.

g. **Freeze any surplus** fish as soon as cooled and wrapped. Mildly smoked fish, such as Scotch Smoked, has very little better keeping quality than fresh fish. If you let it sit in the frig for a time before deciding to freeze it, the fish will have that much *less* shelf life when thawed after freezing.

Resume of Scotch Smoking process

a. Smoke as directed.
b. Dry further without smoking for further firming.
c. Give a 15 minute burst of heat to *polish* fish.
d. Sweat smoked side if further firming needed.
e. Refrigerate for even further firming.
f. Cool fish before wrapping.
g. Freeze surplus immediately.

SERVING SCOTCH SMOKED

Scotch Smoked salmon or trout is best appreciated if served thinly sliced for several reasons: the delicate flavor is most apparent in a thin slice; this product is saltier than hot smoked, so a minimal amount is more pleasant to the palate; lastly, this is an expensive commodity that dictates frugal use.

In Scotland, Ireland and Britain, smoked salmon is traditionally served with buttered brown bread, a lemon wedge, and a grinder of pepper.

You may make up open faced sandwiches for serving, but your guests will probably all have a different taste for *dressing* the smoked salmon or trout. It is gracious to let them make up their own appetizers.

Here are some accompaniments for the slices of smoked fish.

Bread, in addition to whole wheat, may be rye or pumpernickel.

Butter, unsalted is best because of the natural saltiness of the fish.

Cream cheese should be softened with milk or cream.

Onion may be sliced paper thin or grated.

Ham, preferably *country* or *virginia* should be sliced thinly.

Hard cooked egg should be sliced thinly or grated. It can also be mixed with mayonnaise for spreading.

Pepper can be served either in its grinder or coarsely ground in a dish or shaker.

Chapter **9**

Kippering
and Barbecuing

As you have seen earlier, Kippering and Barbecuing are different from Scotch smoking because they are hot smoking processes; the fish is cooked. Scotch Smoked is raw.

Barbecuing

In barbecuing, you have no control over the heat; the smoke is hot only. It is smoke cooking. The fish is placed in a *preheated* smoke oven and kept there until cooked. The only control possible, in some smoke cookers, is having the smoke *on and off* during prolonged cooking.

Kippering

In kippering you gradually bring up the heat to condition the fish before final hot smoking and cooking.

In talking about these two similar processes during the salting-before-smoking instructions, I'll simply call them both kippering. After salting there are separate smoking instruction for both Kippering and Barbecuing.

Whole sides vs pieces for Kippering and Barbecuing

Briefly, you may want to kipper or barbecue a whole side to display at some affair. Generally, pieces of fillets, cut according to thickness, are easier to salt and smoke than full sides (for a full discussion of the subject see chapter 6).

Choice of salting methods

For both whole sides and pieces there are choices of salting methods:

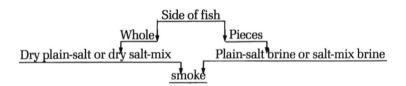

Side of fish

Whole ↓   ↓ Pieces

Dry plain-salt or dry salt-mix   Plain-salt brine or salt-mix brine

smoke

Dry plain salt cure for Kippering

a. **Thick sides** are hard to get drysalted so it is suggested that you *either* cut the side lengthwise into 2 fillets or use a meat pumping needle to inject brine into the thick part of the side (see injecting brine in chapter 8).

b   **Prepare the sides for salting** by scoring the skin as illustrated under Dry-salting for Scotch Smoking (see chapter 8).

c.   *Place the drysalt* as also shown in chapter 8.

Dry plain-salting times for kippering whole sides

Fillet Thickness	Fat Fish	Lean Fish
¾ in.	3 hrs.	1¾ hrs.
1 in.	4 hrs.	2¼ hrs.
1¼ in.	5 hrs.	3 hrs.
1½ in.	6 hrs.	3½ hrs.
*2 in.	† 8 hrs.	† 4½ hrs.
*2½ in.	† 10 hrs.	† 5¾ hrs.
3 in.	† 12 hrs.	† 7 hrs.

d. †   *These times for thicker fillets* are for dry-salting *without* injecting brine into the thick part. If you *inject* brine, cut the times shown by *half*.

e.   *Dry-salting times* for Kippering are considerably less than for Scotch Smoking, as you may have noted. Here is the reason: Scotch Smoked is served thinly sliced, so must be conditioned for slicing by more prolonged salting. Thin slicing is impossible with hot-smoked, kippered fish, so all we want in it is enough salt for flavor. Also, Scotch Smoked is usually consumed in much smaller quantities than kippered; Scotch Smoked is a tidbit · kippered may be a main course.

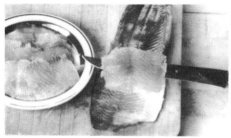 

f.   **Keep a record** of how much salt you used, how long you left it on, and the thickness and estimated fattness of the side. From your record you will be able to duplicate a successful process or improve an inferior one.

g.   *After the dry-salting*, simply rinse the salt off and drain off any surplus water before smoking.

Resume: Dry plain-salting for Kippering

   a.   Cut skin for better salt penetration, and rub salt into cuts.

   b.   Apply salt to fish according to thickness of the flesh. Inject brine into thicker fish.

   c.   Record what you did and its result for future.

   d.   Rinse and drain fish before smoking.

Now turn to Kipper or Barbecue smoking process.

Dry salt-mix (salt-sugar-spice) cure for kippering whole sides

Mix

Pickling Salt		Sugar (white or brown)
18 oz. (2¼ cups)		6 oz. (¾ cup)
	or	
560 g (560 ml)		185 g (185 ml)

a. **Add spices** if you wish. Choose from the following, and adjust the amounts to suit your taste:

Bay leaf	50 leaves, crushed
Pepper	8 tsp. (40 ml)
Mace	2 tbs. (30 ml)
Allspice	7 tsp. (35 ml)
Cloves	2¼ tbs. (34 ml)
Juniper berries	2 tbs. (30 ml) crushed

b. **Prepare the side for salting** as illustrated under Dry-salting for Scotch Smoking (see chapter 8).

c. **Place the dry salt-mix** as also shown in chapter 8.

Dry salt-mix times for kippering whole sides

Fillet Thickness	Fat Fish	Lean Fish
¾ in.	4½ hrs.	2½ hrs.
1 in.	6 hrs.	3½ hrs.
1¼ in.	7½ hrs.	4½ hrs.
1½ in.	9 hrs.	5¾ hrs.
*2 in.	† 12 hrs.	† 6¾ hrs.
*2½ in.	† 15 hrs.	† 9 hrs.
*3 in.	† 18 hrs.	† 10½ hrs.

d. *Thick sides need special consideration; see discussion of them in Plain salt dry-salt cure for kippering

e. †Times for thicker fillets; see discussion of them in Dry plain-salt cure for kippering.

f. **Keep a record**; it will help next time (see Plain salt dry-salt cure for kippering).

g. **After the dry-salt**, rinse off the salt and drain off surplus water before smoking

Resume: Dry salt-mix cure for kippering whole sides

a. Cut skin for better salt penetration and rub salt into cuts.

b. Apply salt-sugar-spice mix according to thickness of the fish. Inject brine into thicker fish.
c. Record what you did and the result for future use.
d. Rinse and drain fish before smoking.

Now turn to Kipper or Barbecue smoking process.

BRINING PIECES FOR KIPPERING

I. Cut fillets into pieces according to the thickness.
II. Choose a brine: either plain salt or salt-sugar-spice.

Plain salt brine for kippering pieces

90 ° Salinometer brine

Pickling Salt	Water
20 oz. (2½ cups)	64 oz.
or	
630 g (630 ml)	2 l

a. **Cool the brine** before using and keep it cool while in use. If you can't keep fish and brine in a cool place (below 50°F - 10°C), put ice in a *watertight* container in the brine. Don't add ice directly to the brine; it will melt, dilute the brine, and throw your brining time off.
b. **Stir pieces** frequently during brining time.

Plain salt brine times for kippering

Thickness	Time
3/8 in.	12 min.
½ in.	24 min.
¾ in.	50 min.
1 in.	65 min.
1¼ in.	1½ hrs.
1½ in.	2 hrs.
2 in.	3 hrs.
3 in.	5 hrs.

c. **Keep a record** of what you did and the result
d. **Drain fish** coming out of the brine, before smoking.

Resume: Plain salt brining pieces before kippering

a. Cut fillets into pieces according to thickness.
b. Make 90° Sal. plain salt brine.
c. Brine, using table as a guide.
d. Drain fish before smoking.
e. Record times and results.

Now turn to Kipper or Barbecue smoking process.

Salt-mix (salt - sugar - spice) brine for kippering pieces

Salt-mix Brine

Pickling Salt	Sugar (white or brown)	Water
36 oz. (4½ cups)	12 oz. (1½ cups)	128 oz.
	or	
1120 g (1120 ml)	370 g (370 ml)	4 l

a. **Add spices,** if you wish, from the following; adjust the amounts to suit your taste:

Bay leaf	50 leaves, crushed
Pepper	8 tsp. (40 ml)
Mace	2 tbs. (30 ml)
Allspice	7 tsp. (35 ml)
cloves	2¼ tbs. (34 ml)
Juniper berries	2 tbs. (30 ml) crushed

b. **Simmer spices** in the brine for 45 minutes, then strain through a cloth lined strainer or funnel. Discard the spices.
c. **Cool the brine** and keep it cool (see Plain salt brining for kippering.
d. **Stir pieces** frequently after placing in brine.

Salt-mix brine times for kippering

Thickness	Time
3/8 in.	10 min.
½ in.	20 min.
¾ in.	45 min.
1 in.	60 min.
1¼ in.	1¼ hrs.

1½ in.	1¾ hrs.
2 in.	2½ hrs.
3 in.	4½ hrs.

e. **Keep a record** (see Dry-salting for kippering).

f. **Drain fish** coming out of the brine before smoking.

Resume: Salt-mix brining pieces before kippering
a. Cut fillets into pieces according to thickness.
b. Make salt-sugar-spice brine.
c. Brine using tables as a guide.
d. Drain fish before smoking
e. Record times and results.

Now turn to Kipper or Barbecue smoking process

REUSING BRINES

With today's high cost of ingredients you may wish to re-use the brines it you're doing a lot of smoking. If so, *it is imperative* that you bring the brine back up to strength before using it again. This is necessary because the fish has taken salt and sugar *out* of the brine and put water *in*.

To reconstitute a used brine use a salinometer (*see footnote) to determine the brine's strength then add enough salt or salt-sugar mix to bring it back to its original strength.

The following tables show how much salt or salt and sugar mix to add after reading the salinometer.

Salt-sugar mix to reconstitute a salt-sugar brine

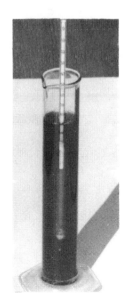

Salt	Sugar
2 parts	1 part
by weight or volume	by weight or volume

To reconstitute, add dry mix according to salinometer reading:

Salinometer reading	To 128 oz. brine add dry mix	To 4 l brine add dry mix
70° Sal.	14 oz. (1¾ cups)	420 g (420 ml)
80° Sal.	7 oz. (7/8 cup)	210 g (210 ml)

Plain-salt brine reconstitution

Salinometer reading	To 128 oz. brine add dry mix	To 4 l brine add dry mix
70° Sal.	11 oz. (22 tbs.)	340 g (340 ml)
80° Sal.	5½ oz. (11 tbs.)	170 g (170 ml)

*Get your salinometer from a laboratory supply house, or order it from your hardware store.

SMOKING KIPPERED SALMON

Dry first

Drying is important to good appearance and flavor. During drying, the salt soluble protein from the fish forms a *skin* on the surface of the fish called the pellicle. During smoking, the smoke combines with the pellicle and gives the fish a pleasant smoked appearance and most of its smoke flavor.

How to dry

Drying is a major problem for most home smokers. I have read a number of suggestions for drying including: hang the fish under the eaves of a building (out of the sun) in a breeze; turn a fan on the fish, etc. If you are using a *smoke cooker*, you must rely on a breeze or a fan for drying the fish. If you are using a *natural-draft* smoker, you can light a small clear fire (unsmoky) and create a draft of warm air that will dry the fish right in the smoker. If you are using a forced-draft smoker, you of course have the forced draft to also do the drying in the smoker.

Tempering is also important

Tempering is *gradual* as opposed to *sudden* heating, and is also important both for appearance and quality. Sudden heating is undesirable because it brings soluble protein (juice) to the surface where it forms pools on the surface. The pools then dry into white, unappetizing *curds* as the fish smokes. Sudden heating also causes cracks in the surface and uneven drying.

Kippering vs. Barbecueing

The ability of your smoker to *gradually* bring the fish up to heat separates *kippering* from *barbecueing*. If you can't control the heat - bring it up gradually - turn to the barbecueing instructions.

Note the glossy pellicle on well dried fillets for smoking

Curds formed by rapid heating during hot smoking

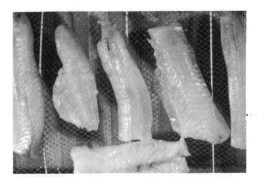

Kippered smoking process

Smoking conditions are the same for either a natural or forced - draft smoker, except for the drying phase.

Drying

Temperature .... 100° F - (38° C)
Draft .... as much as possible
Time: (Forced-draft) .... 1½ hrs.
    (Natural-draft) .... 3 to 4 hrs. - depends on weather

First smoking

Temperature .... 100° F - (38° C)
Smoke .... medium density
Time .... 1 hr.

Tempering

Temperature .... gradually raise temp. to 175° F - (80° C)
Smoke .... medium density
Time .... take 1 hr. to reach maximum temperature

More smoking

Temperature .... 175° F - (80° C)
Smoke .... medium density
Time. .... 1 hr.

Take *thinner* pieces out of the smoker now and continue smoking the *thicker* ones for 1 more hour under the same conditions as the last hour.

Barbecuing or Smoke-cooking process

Smoking and cooking

Continue smoking and cooking until the fish is cooked. The usual method of testing (trying from time to time until the fish flakes) is as good as any. Thick fish naturally take longer to cook, so if you are using a creosotey wood such as alder, you may want to smoke only part of the cooking time. This is possible, of course, only if your smoke-cooker has a source of heat other than a fire; a hotplate for example.

Cool fish quickly

Cool your kippered or barbecued fish as soon as possible, and certainly before wrapping it. If you wrap it before it is thoroughly cooled, it will soon spoil.

In a forced-draft smoker, simply shunt the smoke to the outside, turn off the heat, and let the cool air efficiently do the cooling job.

Get fish out of other smokers immediately, and *spread* it out to cool.

Freeze surplus quickly

Freeze any surplus fish as soon as it cools. Kippered fish has very little better refrigerator life than fresh. If you let fish sit around for days before freezing, after thawing it will have that many fewer days of life left.

Chapter **10**

Recipes for kippered fish

I didn't know how exciting fish dishes could be when made with smoked fish, until introduced to the idea when traveling abroad. My introduction came at the Cleikum Grill of the North British Hotel, Edinburgh; the dish was Ham and Hadie, grilled with smoked ham, and served with the combined juices poured over mashed potatoes. So, to introduce this chapter I'll start with a simple dish that reminds me of it - Country Pot.

Country Pot

½ lb. hot smoked salmon or trout (225 g)	2 tbs. butter (30 ml)
¼ lb. cooked ham (115 g)	chopped parsley
6 medium potatoes	pepper
1 small onion	

Peel and quarter the potatoes and barely cover them with unsalted water. Slice the onion and sprinkle over the potatoes. Cook the potatoes until about 2/3 done.

Place the flaked fish, and the ham - cut into ½ inch (12 mm) cubes - on the potatoes and continue cooking until potatoes are tender and the fish and ham are warmed through.

Serve the potatoes, ham, and fish with the broth from the pot. Sprinkle parsley, and dots of butter over all.

Serves 4.

Smoky

1 lb. hot smoked salmon or trout (450 g)	¼ cup swiss cheese (grated) (60 ml)
1 cup heavy cream (240 ml)	2 tbs. parmesan (grated) (30 ml)
2 medium tomatoes	freshly ground pepper

Flake the fish and spread it in a buttered, shallow baking dish.

Pour ½ cup of the cream over the fish.

Dice the tomatoes and spread over cream and fish, season with pepper.

Pour the other ½ cup of cream over the tomatoes, and sprinkle with the cheese.

Bake at 350° F for 20 minutes, then brown the top for a minute under the broiler.

Serves 4.

Potato Scallop

¾ lb. **hot** smoked salmon
    or trout (340 g)
2 cups pototoes cooked, sliced (480 ml)
1 tbs. grated onion (15 ml)
salt, pepper

1 cup thin white sauce or
    creamed soup (240 ml)
½ cup dry bread crumbs (120 ml)
1 tbs. butter (15 ml

Arrange alternate layers of sliced potatoes, onion and flaked fish in a buttered casserole. Season each layer with salt and pepper.

Add the white sauce to the casserole, sprinkle bread crumbs over and dot with butter.

Bake at 375° F for 20 minutes or until browned.

Serves 6.

Chowder

1/3 lb. hot smoked salmon
    or trout (150 g)
1 cup cream of potato, celery,
    or mushroom soup
1 cup milk (240 ml)
pepper

1 tbs. chopped parsley (15 ml)

dill weed

salt

Heat soup and milk to boiling.

Flake and add fish.

Season with dill, and freshly ground pepper, and salt if necessary and cook 5 minutes.

Serve with chopped parsley.

Serves 2 or 3.

Romanoff

1 lb. **hot** smoked salmon
    or trout (450 g)
2 cups sour cream (480 ml)
1 cup cottage cheese (240 ml)
6 oz. noodles (170 g)

1 clove garlic (chopped)

2 tbs. butter (30 ml)
tabasco to taste
1 cup shredded cheddar
    cheese (240 ml)

Place cottage cheese and sour cream in a bowl, season with tabasco.

Saute onions and garlic in butter until onions are transparent, add to cheese in bowl.

Flake and add salmon to bowl.

Cook noodles by package directions, drain and mix with other ingredients.

Place mixture in a buttered 8 inch (20 cm) baking dish and sprinkle with the cheddar.

Bake in a preheated 325° F oven for 30 minutes.

Serves 6.

Quiche

¼ lb. hot smoked salmon
    or trout (112 g)
½ lb. cream cheese (225 g)
5 eggs
1 cup heavy cream (240 ml)
½ tsp. dijon mustard (3 ml)

½ cup minced onion (120 ml)

1 tbs. butter (15 ml)
1 tbs. lemon rind (grated) (15 ml)
salt
pepper

One recipe *rich* pie dough (preferably made with sweet butter) - enough for a 9 in. (23 cm) pie shell.

Prepare the pie dough and put it in to bake.

Soften the cream cheese. Beat the eggs *slightly* - reserve enough of the beaten eggs to glaze the bottom of the baked pie shell (1 - 2 tbs.). Mix the beaten eggs, cream, and cream cheese, mustard, lemon rind, salt, and freshly ground pepper.

Saute the onions in the butter until soft, then add flaked salmon to pan and stir gently until salmon warms and absorbs butter.

Brush the baked pie shell with the egg mix and put it into the oven to glaze (1 - 2 minutes).

Arrange the salmon - onion mix in the shell and pour the cream - egg mix over it.

Bake at 350° F for 30 minutes or until quiche passes the custard *clean knife* test in the middle.

Cool to lukewarm before serving.

Serves 6.

Casserole Florentine

1 lb. hot smoked salmon
    or trout (450 g)
1½ cups cooked drained
    spinach (360 ml)
1 tbs. melted butter (15 ml)
¼ tsp. pepper (1.5 ml)

1/8 tsp. nutmeg (.75 ml)
2 tbs. chopped onion (30 ml)
1 tbs. cooking oil (15 ml)

3 tbs. flour (45 ml)

1¼ cups milk or fish stock (300 ml)

2 tbs. sherry (30 ml
¼ cup parmesan cheese,
    grated (60 ml)
3 hard cooked eggs, sliced
1 clove finely chopped garlic
watercress or parsley

Chop spinach, put in bottom of greased baking dish; season with melted butter, pepper, and nutmeg.

Cook onion and garlic in butter until tender; blend in flour; add milk or fish stock and cook until thick, stirring constantly.

Break up and mash the smoked fish; add it and sherry to the sauce, and blend with an electric mixer or blender; pour over the spinach.

Sprinkle with grated cheese and bake in a 350° F oven for 20 to 25 minutes.

Garnish with egg slices and watercress or parsley.

Serves 6.

Pilaf

1 lb. **hot** smoked salmon or trout (450 g)	1 chopped medium onion
1 cup raw white rice (240 ml)	1 clove garlic, minced
2 cups chicken broth (480 ml)	2 tbs. chopped parsley (30 ml)
½ cup butter or margarine (120 ml)	¼ tsp. saffron or tumeric (1.5 ml)

Melt butter in a heavy casserole or baking dish.
Saute onion, garlic, saffron until transparent.
Add rice and stir to coat with butter.
Add chicken broth.
Bring liquid to a boil.
Flake and add salmon, stir to mix, cover.
Bake in a preheated 400° F oven for 30 minutes.
Fluff rice and sprinkle with parsley.

Curry

1 lb. hot smoked salmon or trout (450 g)	¼ tsp. salt (1 + ml)
¼ cup chopped onion (60 ml)	¼ tsp. ginger (1 + ml)
3 tbs. butter or oil (45 ml)	pepper
3 tbs. flour (45 ml)	2 cups milk (480 ml)
1½ tsp. curry powder (7 ml)	3 cups cooked rice (720 ml)

Cook onion in the butter or oil, blend in the flour and seasonings.
Add the milk and cook while stirring constantly until thick.
Add the flaked or chunked fish and heat.
Serve over the rice with any or all the these curry condiments:

chopped green pepper	toasted shredded coconut
chopped canton ginger	sieved hard cooked eggs
chopped tomatoes	chopped nuts
chopped onions	

Serves 6.

French Hot Mousse

1½ lb. **cold** or **hot** smoked salmon or trout (675 g)	½ tsp. dry mustard (3 ml)
1 tbs. butter (15 ml)	1/8 tsp. nutmeg (1 ml)
½ tbs. flour (8 ml)	3 oz. milk (90 ml)
pepper to taste	2 eggs separated
1 oz. cognac (30 ml)	1 cup whipping cream (250 ml)

Grind cold smoked fish finely or mash and blend hot smoked fish.

Melt butter in a saucepan; blend in flour, pepper, mustard, nutmeg.

Gradually add milk, stirring steadily until it comes to a boil; lower heat and cook for 5 minutes.

Beat cognac with egg yolks and gradually add a *little* hot sauce to egg yolk. Add warmed egg yolk mixture to sauce stirring steadily.

Whip egg whites and cream separately.

Mix fish into sauce, then fold in egg whites, and whipped cream.

Turn into a buttered casserole, place in a shallow pan of hot water, and bake in a preheated 350° F oven for 50 minutes or until firm.

Serve with a sauce.

Serves 4 to 6.

Souffle

½ lb. hot smoked salmon or trout (227 g)	¼ cup butter or margarine
6 eggs separated	½ tsp. dry mustard (3 ml)
1 cup milk (240 ml)	1 tbs. chopped parsley (15 ml)
¼ cup flour (60 ml)	dash cayenne

Beat yolks.

Melt butter, blend in flour and seasonings, add milk gradually and cook with constant stirring.

Stir a little of the hot sauce into the egg yolks, then add yolks to the remaining sauce stirring constantly.

Flake salmon, add it and parsley to the sauce.

Beat egg whites until stiff.

Fold salmon mixture into the egg whites.

Pour into a well greased 2 quart casserole.

Bake in a 350° F oven for 45 minutes or until souffle is firm in the center.

Serves 6.

Stuffed Baked Potatoes

¾ lb. hot smoked salmon or trout	1 egg, beaten
6 baking potatoes	¼ cup onion, finely chopped (60 ml)
½ cup hot milk (120 ml)	¼ cup parsley finely chopped (60 ml)
¼ tsp. pepper, freshly ground (1.5 ml)	½ cup fine bread crumbs (120 ml)
¼ tsp. thyme (1.5 ml)	¼ cup butter, melted (60 ml)

Bake potatoes as usual, cut in half lengthwise while hot. Carefully scoop potato out of shells - keep shells intact for stuffing.

Mash potato, add hot milk and beat until fluffy.

Flake and mash fish and add it, parsley, and onion to potatoes.

Beat egg and seasonings together and combine with mix - fold all together.

Heap mixture into potato shells.

Mix bread crumbs with butter, and sprinkle over potatoes.

Bake 20 minutes at 350° F or until browned.

Serves 6.

Battered with Shrimp and/or Mussels

1½ lb. **hot** smoked salmon
    or trout (675 g)
3 tbs. melted butter (45 ml)
freshly ground pepper
1 tbs. lemon rind, grated (15 ml)
4 tsp. parsley, finely chopped (20 ml)

4 tsp. fresh chopped chervil,
    basil or tarragon (20 ml)
or ½ tsp. (2.5 ml) dried
4 tbs. melted butter (60 ml)
    optional
1 cup cooked shrimp or steamed
    mussels (240 ml)

Batter

1 cup flour (240 ml)
2 eggs

2½ cups milk (640 ml)

Break fish into bite size chunks and arrange in a buttered baking dish. Season with pepper, and lemon rind, and sprinkle with the chosen herb and parsley.

Pour melted butter over fish and toss until fish is well coated.

Sprinkle with shrimps or mussels.

Batter Making

Sift flour into a mixing bowl, and make a well in the center.

Break 1 egg into the well and mix into flour, then stir in *half* of the milk.

Stir in remaining egg and beat till smooth; gradually beat in remaining milk.

Let the batter stand for at least 1 hour.

Pour batter over fish and bake at 375° F until the batter has risen, is brown and firm.

Serve immediately.

Serves 6.

Biscuit Roll

1 lb. **hot** smoked salmon
    or trout (450 g)
¼ cup cream of chicken soup (60 ml)
2 cup batch of biscuit dough (480 ml)
2/3 cup milk (160 ml)
2 tbs. butter or margarine (30 ml)
½ cup chopped celery (120 ml)

½ cup chopped green pepper (120 ml)
¼ cup minced onion (60 ml)
½ cup chopped ripe olives (120 ml)
1 egg
1 tbs. water (15 mm)

Saute vegetables in butter until soft, then stir in olives.

Flake salmon and add to vegetables, stir in the chicken soup.

Make biscuit dough, turn out on floured board, knead gently about 12 times.

Roll dough to a 9 × 12 inch (22 × 30 cm) rectangle.

Spread salmon mix on dough and roll up lengthwise like a jelly roll.

Combine egg and water and brush mix on roll.

Bake in a preheated 400° F oven for 25 to 30 minutes or until light brown.

Slice and serve with your favorite sauce.

Cornbread

1 lb. **hot** smoked salmon
or trout (227 g)
1 cup milk (240 ml)
¼ cup melted shortening
or butter (60 ml)
1 egg, beaten

1 - 2 tbs. sugar (15 - 30 ml)

¾ cup sifted flour (180 ml)
1¼ cup corn meal (300 ml)

4 tsp. baking powder (20 ml)

Flake fish
Sift together corn meal, flour, baking powder, sugar.
Combine egg, milk, shortening.
Add liquid to other ingredients and mix just enough to moisten.
Stir in salmon.
Place in a well greased 8 X 8 X 2 inch baking dish and bake in a 425° F oven for 25 to 30 minutes.
Serves 6.

Russian Kotlets

2 lbs. hot smoked salmon
or trout (900 g)
1 cup white bread, soaked in milk
and squeezed out (240 ml)
1 egg, beaten
bread crumbs

4 oz. butter (120 ml)

1 cup frying oil (240 ml)

pepper to taste

Mash or chop the fish finely and add the soaked bread, egg, and pepper.
Roll tablespoons of the mix into balls.
Insert ½ tsp. (2½ ml) of butter into the middle of each ball, then flatten the ball to a ½ inch (1.25 cm) thick kotlet.
Roll kotlets in bread crumbs and fry in oil.
Serve with a sauce or salad.
Serves 6.

Turkish Croquettes

½ lb. **hot** smoked salmon
or trout (450 g)
1 slice white bread
2 eggs
2 tbs. chopped parsley (30 ml)
2 tbs. chopped fresh dill (30 ml)
oil for frying

2 green onions, chopped (tops & all)

2 tbs. black currants (30 ml)
2 tbs. chopped walnuts (30 ml)
½ tsp. allspice (2.5 ml)
½ cup flour (120 ml)
pepper

Flake fish into mixing bowl.
Moisten bread in water and squeeze out excess.
Add bread, eggs, onions, parsley, dill, currants, walnuts, and seasonings.
Mash with a fork to a paste, and roll into croquettes about 2½ inches long.
Roll croquettes in flour and fry in oil until golden brown all over.
Serves 4.

Norwegian Farce

1 lb. hot smoked salmon	white pepper
or trout (450 g)	salt
5 tbs. potato or wheat flour (75 ml)	2 oz. butter (60 ml)
2 eggs	
1 qt. ½ & ½ cream	
(may not need all) (1 l)	

Flake fish and use a blender or mincer to reduce it to a paste.

Work in the softened butter with your hands, then work in the eggs one at a time, then gradually mix in the cream until the paste is of a good consistency for shaping into small balls. It the farce curdles place the bowl in hot water and whip it smooth again.

Bring 1 qt. (1 l) salted water to a boil, shape farce into ball with 2 spoons dipped in hot water.

Cook 1 ball for 10 minutes to check its consistency, if too stiff add more cream, if too soft add more egg. Cook, a few at a time, for 10 minutes.

Serve with your favorite fish sauce.

Serves 4.

Brandade

1½ lb. hot smoked salmon	juice of ½ lemon
or trout (675 ml)	freshly ground pepper
1 clove garlic, crushed	toast triangles
½ cup whipping cream (120 ml)	
½ cup olive oil (120 ml)	

Flake fish, place it in a blender or food processor; add garlic, 2 tbs. (30 ml) cream, and 4 tbs. (60 ml) olive oil and blend; add cream and olive oil alternately until they are both absorbed and brandade is creamy smooth.

Before serving, simmer brandade in a double boiler; stir in lemon juice and ground pepper.

Serve hot or cold on toast triangles that have been fried in olive oil.

Serves 4 to 6.

Fried Sandwiches

½ lb. **hot** smoked salmon	½ tbs. green onion
or trout (225 g)	(finely chopped) (8 ml)
2 eggs well beaten	1/5 tsp. dried tarragon (crushed) (1 ml)
½ cup milk (120 ml)	1/5 tsp. salt (1 ml)
¼ cup sour cream (60 ml)	1 tsp. prepared mustard (5 ml)
¼ cup celery (finely chopped) (60 ml)	8 slices of bread
½ tsp. prepared horseradish (3 ml)	¼ cup shortening (120 ml)
sesame seeds	pepper

Flake the fish finely into a mixing bowl.

Combine the beaten eggs and milk.

Blend together the salmon, sour cream, celery, horseradish, green onion mustard, tarragon, salt and pepper.

Divide the salmon mixture between four slices of bread and cover with the remaining four slices.

Dip the sandwiches into the egg mixture, sprinkle with sesame seeds and fry in the shortening, on both sides, until brown

Potato or Macaroni Salad

1 lb. **hot** smoked salmon or trout (450 g)	2 tbs. minced parsley (30 ml)
	1 tbs. dried dill weed (15 ml)
6 cups cooked, diced potatoes or macaroni (1440 ml)	¼ tsp. pepper (1.5 ml)
	2 tbs. lemon juice (30 ml)
½ cup chopped green onions (120 ml)	12 cherry tomatoes
1 cup diced cucumber (240 ml)	12 cucumber slices
1 cup chopped celery (240 ml)	parsley garnish
2 cups mayonnaise (480 ml)	
¼ cup milk (50 ml)	

Flake salmon and mix with potatoes (or macaroni), green onions, cucumber, celery, minced parsley, and dill weed.

Combine mayonnaise, milk, pepper, and lemon juice, and pour over salmon mixture.

Toss salad gently, pack into a 10 cup mold or deep bowl, and chill.

Unmold to serve, and garnish with cucumber slices, tomatoes, and parsley.

Russian Salad

1 lb. **hot** smoked salmon or trout (450 g)	½ tsp. celery salt (2 ml)
½ cup sour cream (120 ml)	2 tsp. chopped parsley (10 ml)
2 tbs. green onion, chopped (30 ml)	lettuce leaves
pepper freshly ground	

Break salmon into bite size pieces and add sour cream, onion, celery salt, and parsley; season with pepper.

Serve in lettuce cups.

Serves 4.

Scandinavian Salad

½ lb. hot or cold smoked salmon or trout (225 g)	2 medium potatoes, boiled, chilled, and sliced
¼ lb. fresh mushrooms, sliced (112 g)	¼ cup lemon juice (60 ml)
4 hard cooked eggs, sliced	½ cup salad oil (120 ml)
freshly ground pepper	½ tsp. dried dill weed (3 ml)
1/8 tsp. salt (1 ml)	

Serves 6 at luncheon.

Make a dressing out of the salad oil, lemon juice, salt and pepper. Pour the dressing over the potato slices and marinate for at least 10 minutes.

Drain the potatoes and reserve the dressing. Arrange the potatoes, sliced mushrooms, sliced eggs and flaked salmon on torn lettuce leaves in a cool salad bowl; sprinkle with the dill weed.

Toss with reserved dressing and lift into individual salad bowls.

Tartelettes

For a special presentation make the tartelette shells by using a scallop shell as a mold. Butter the *back* side of the shell and using the same dough as for the quiche (rolled out to 1/8 in. - 3 mm thickness) *form* the dough over the buttered back of the shell, and use your fingers to cut off the excess on the sharp edge of the shell. In cutting the dough off, leave a little excess and form this over the edge of the shell so the dough will stay in place during the baking. Brush with a beaten whole - egg wash and bake in a 400° F oven for 30 minutes or until browned. Work the baked *shell* loose from the shell mold with your fingers, brush the inside with the egg wash and glaze in the oven for a minute or two.

Tartelette Filling

Flake *hot* smoked salmon or trout into a cream sauce, preferably made with heavy cream. Be generous with the fish.

Place creamed fish in the tartelettes, cover with mornay sauce (traditionally made with Swiss cheese but excellent with cheddar).

Sprinkle the filling with grated cheese, and bake in a 400° F oven to brown and melt cheese. Serve Hot.

Alternate Tartelettes

Form quiche dough into small molds or muffin tins, and bake in a 400° F oven for 30 minutes or until brown, then handle like *scallop* shells.

East Indian Appetizers

1 lb. **hot** smoked salmon or trout (450 g)	3 tbs. chopped parsley (45 ml)
2 potatoes	1 green chili, seeded and chopped
vegetable oil for deep frying	salt to taste
1 onion, chopped	2 tbs. lemon juice (30 ml)
4 cloves garlic, crushed	flour
¼ tsp. tumeric (1.5 ml)	lemon slices
½ tsp. grated ginger (2.5 ml)	

Boil and mash potatoes, flake and mash fish, combine the two.

Fry onion and garlic, in sufficient oil, for 5 minutes; add tumeric, ginger, parsley, and chili; fry 1 minute more. Add potato - fish mix, salt and lemon juice, stir and cook for 2 or 3 minutes, cool.

Roll mixture into 1 inch (2.5 cm) balls, roll in flour, deep fry at 375° F (190° C) until brown.

Serve hot with lemon slices.

Makes about 20 balls.

Appetizers with Crepes

10 precooked 6 to 8 in. crepes
½ lb. **hot** smoked salmon
    or trout (112 g)
8 oz. cream cheese softened (225 g)
¼ cup green pepper finely
    chopped (60 ml)
½ cup sour cream (120 ml)

2 tsp. milk (10 ml)
1 tbs. grated onion (15 ml)

¼ tsp. garlic powder (1.5 ml)
salt and freshly ground pepper

Mix milk, cream cheese, sour cream, garlic powder, salt and pepper to taste, grated onion, flaked fish, and green pepper.

Spread one tenth of mixture on a crepe, then cover with another crepe, alternating crepes and spread until 5 crepes high.

Make 2 stacks like this, then cut into small pie - shaped wedges for serving. Refrigerate before serving.

Makes 16 to 20 wedges.

II

5 precooked 6 to 8 in. crepes
¼ lb. **hot** smoked salmon
    or trout (120 g)
3 oz. cream cheese, softened (85 g)
2 tbs. mayonnaise (30 ml)

1 tbs. chopped chives (15 ml)
1 tbs. green pepper or pimento,
finely chopped (15 ml)
freshly ground pepper

Mix the cream cheese, mayonnaise, chives, peppers, finely flaked fish together until smooth, and season with pepper.

Spread one fifth of the mixture on each crepe.

Cut crepes into pie - shaped wedges, and roll up each wedge.

They can be served hot or cold. If served cold, refrigerate well before serving.

Makes about 25.

III

6 precooked 6 to 8 in. crepes
¼ lb. **cold** smoked salmon or
    salmon, thinly sliced (120 g)
3 oz. cream cheese, softened (85 g)
2 tbs. sour cream (30 ml)

½ tbs. prepared horseradish (7 ml)
1 tbs. chopped chives (15 ml)

freshly ground pepper

Mix cream cheese, sour cream, horseradish, and chives, and season with pepper.

Spread one sixth of the mix on each crepe, and cover with the fish slices.

Roll each crepe and cut rolls diagonally first one way then the other to make wedge shaped individual rolls. Refrigerate before serving.

Makes about 30.

Soused

½ lb. hot or cold smoked salmon or trout (240 ml)	2/3 cup sour cream (160 ml)
1 tsp. peppercorns (5 ml)	1 tsp. Dijon mustard (5 ml)
½ tsp. dill seed (2.5 ml)	lemon juice
1 bay leaf	salt
1¼ cups dry white wine (360 ml)	4 tsp. chopped chives (20 ml)
1 sliced dill pickle	

Flake or slice salmon into a covered glass dish. Sprinkle with peppercorns and dill seed; add bay leaf and cover with wine; refrigerate overnight.

When ready to serve drain marinade from the fish, strain half of marinade into a bowl.

Add sour cream and mustard to the marinade and flavor to taste with lemon juice and salt if necessary.

Serve fish covered with sauce and garnished with pickle slices and chopped chives

Serves 4.

Stuffed Artichoke Appetizers

1 lb. hot or cold smoked salmon or trout (450 g)	mornay sauce
1 lb. spinach (450 g)	grated Swiss or Cheddar cheese
12 artichoke hearts small to medium size	

Cook artichoke hearts and keep warm.

Place half of the fish on the hearts, cover with the spinach which has been cooked, pressed dry, and chopped. Place remaining half of fish on the spinach.

Cover the filling with mornay sauce, sprinkle with the grated cheese and bake in a 350° F oven until filling is warmed and the topping is browned.

Pate d' Amiens

Court Bouillon

½ cup dry white wine (120 ml)	½ small carrot, sliced
½ tbs. salt (7 ml)	¼ medium onion, sliced
4 peppercorns	water
½ rib celery, sliced	1 small bay leaf

Dough

2 cups flour (all purpose) (480 ml)	1 tsp. salt (5 ml)
½ lb. unsalted butter (225 g)	½ cup cold water (120 ml)

Pate

1 lb. white fish fillets (450 g)	¼ tsp. ground nutmeg (1.5 ml)
1 lb. hot or cold smoked salmon or trout (450 g)	¼ cup heavy cream (60 ml)

½ cup butter (softened) (250 g)   ¼ tsp. chervil (1.5 ml)
½ tsp. salt (3 ml)   1 tsp. tarragon (5 ml)
½ tsp. pepper freshly ground (3 ml) 4 tbs. butter (60 ml)
1 egg yolk   8 large mushroom caps

Mixing Dough

Mix flour, salt, and butter together in a bowl until crumbly.

Add enough water (more than ½ cup if necessary), and mix until it forms a ball - stop mixing immediately - don't overwork; then let it rest for 30 minutes on a lightly floured board.

Roll dough out into a square (about a foot square - 30 cm²). Fold 1/3 of the square over the middle third then the other 1/3 over the first and let rest for 10 minutes covered with a floured towel.

Roll dough out again to a 12 X 12 in. (30 X 30 cm) square, again fold the side thirds over the middle; cover with the floured towel until you're ready to use.

Poaching the White Fish

Place the seasonings and vegetables in a saucepan, add enough water to just cover, and boil for 20 minutes.

Pour stock and vegetables into the poaching pan, add wine then the fillets and if necessary more water to cover fish.

Bring up to just *below* a simmer and poach fish for 10 minutes per inch (2.5 cm) of thickness; remove fish.

Making the Pate

Skin the fillets if necessary and place them and mushroom caps in a food processor or blender; *puree* the mixture.

Put mixture into a bowl along with the softened butter and mix with your hands.

Add the salt, pepper, nutmeg and cream; mix to a spreadable paste.

Roll the folded dough out into a rectangle.

Spread *half* of the fish paste in the centre 1/3 of the dough.

Break up or cut up the smoked salmon or trout and distribute the pieces on the fish paste.

Melt the 4 tbs. of butter and add the chervil and tarragon; mix and pour over the pieces of smoked fish.

Spread the last half of the fish paste over the smoked fish.

Fold one side of the uncovered dough over the fish, then the second un-covered side over the first, moisten the edge of the top, fold and seal. Roll up ends and turn the loaf *over* on a foil covered cookie sheet; make a vent hole in the centre about 1 in. (25 mm) in diameter.

Brush with the egg yolk mixed with water and bake in a preheated 400° F oven until golden brown - about 15 minutes; lower the oven to 350° F and bake for 45 minutes longer.

Slice and serve hot.

Serves 4.

German Cold Mousse (Lachscreme)

1 lb. **hot** smoked salmon
   or trout (450 g)

1 tbs. butter (15 ml)
1 tbs. finely chopped onion (15 ml)
1 tbs. flour (15 ml)
½ cup warm milk (120 ml)
1 cup whipping cream (240 ml)

1 truffle or few black olives or a
   caper and celery stalk (see
   direction for The Aspic)
1 envelope geletin
   (concentrated) (120 ml)
1/3 cup sherry (80 ml)

½ cup water (120 ml)

1 pinch cayenne
½ tsp. anchovy paste (3 ml)
salt
pepper
1 tbs. fresh dill (15 ml)
   (1 tsp. dried - 5 ml)
¼ cup pistachio nuts (60 ml)
   (finely chopped)

½ cup chicken broth

Mousse

Flake fish and make it into a paste in a mortar, blender or processor.

Heat butter in a saucepan and add onion; when butter bubbles add flour and stir for 5 minutes taking care not to brown. Take pan off heat and stir in the warm milk. Cook and stir sauce over low heat until it thickens.

Add cayenne and anchovy paste to sauce and stir sauce into the fish paste. Season with salt and freshly ground pepper. Add the dill and pistachio nuts, blend all together and chill.

Aspic

Put the envelope of gelatin in ½ cup (120 ml) cold water to soften. Bring the chicken broth and sherry to a boil and remove from heat. Let chicken - sherry mix cool slightly then add the gelatin and mix, then cool the aspic.

The Mold

Place a 1 qt. (1 l.) fish mold, or other suitable container, in cracked ice. Coat the bottom and sides with cooled but still liquid aspic; a soft pastry brush is good for building up a coating on the sides. Let this first layer set well.

On the bottom of the mold (if it is a fish mold; any other kind of mold, skip this step) lay a round piece of truffel, or a black olive half, or a caper on the bottom aspic, for the eye of the fish. For the lateral line (center line) of the fish, lay half slices of ripe olives, or crescent shaped slices of truffel; or thin slices of celery stalk, to give a scale - like representation.

Pour a second layer, to just cover the decorations, on the first, and paint the sides until there is at least a ½ in (13 mm) layer of aspic on them.

Chill the rest of the aspic to use in the final serving.

Whip the cream with just a pinch of salt, and carefully blend it into the fish paste until just smooth. Pour it into the mold, and chill for at least 2 hours before serving.

Use a platter for serving that is large enough to leave a generous amount of room around the mold. Unmold the mousse (see unmolding technique for Jelled Cooked Marinades in chapter 20) on to the platter and surround with such decorations as marinated shrimps, stuffed eggs, tomato wedges, parsley tufts, etc.

Now unmold the remaining aspic, and cut it into slices, then continue cutting the slices into dice using a twisting motion with knife - cut to fairly small dice. Now spoon this *sparkley* dice around the mousse and other accompaniments.

Serve with green mayonnaise.

Serves 4.

Danish Omelet

¼ lb. hot or cold smoked salmon
    or trout (112 g)
6 large eggs
½ cup milk (120 ml)
1 tsp. potato or corn flour (5 ml)
2 medium tomatoes cut in wedges

pepper, freshly ground

1 tbs. butter (15 ml)
sliced radishes
chopped chives

Beat eggs with the milk and flour and season with pepper.

Melt butter in pan and pour in omelet mix.

Flake fish, and when omelet is beginning to set, distribute the fish on it.

Place tomato wedges, and sliced radishes on omelet, and sprinkle chopped chives over.

Serve immediately when cooked.

Serves 6.

Norwegian Eggs

buttered bread
cold or hot smoked salmon or trout
chopped chives

scrambled eggs
chopped dill

Place thinly sliced fish on buttered bread, cover with scrambled eggs, and garnish with chopped dill and/or chives.

English Scrambled Eggs

½ lb. **hot** smoked salmon
    or trout (225 g)
4 slices decrusted bread
3 tbs. cooking oil (45 ml)
2 oz. butter (60 ml)

4 eggs

4 tbs. milk (60 ml)
1 tbs. chopped parsley (15 ml)
pepper

Cut slices of bread into 1 inch (2.5 cm) squares and fry until golden in the cooking oil and 2 tbs. (30 ml) of the butter. Keep warm.

Beat eggs, milk, parsley, and pepper and stir in the flaked fish.

Melt the remaining butter in a frying pan, pour in egg mix, cook with constant stirring over low heat until the eggs are set. Stir in the toasted bread just before serving.

Serves 4.

Chapter **11**

Making Lox

Please read about Lox in chapter 8.

In chapter 8 you have seen that there are three different products called Lox (plus a lot of smoked and pickled products using the name but bearing no resemblance to any of the three).

The three products discussed here are:

1. Lox (old fashioned)
2. Nova Lox
3. Lox Salmon

HOW TO MAKE
OLD FASHIONED LOX

In chapter 23 I describe how to make Mild Cured Salmon or Trout. If they have been in the cure between 2 and 52 weeks (under 2, not cured - over 52, too old) you are ready to proceed.

Freshening comes first. In the mild salting instructions it was strongly suggested that the fillet be divided into pieces according to thickness. This is important now that we are ready to freshen, because obviously the thick and thin parts will freshen at different rates. If the thin parts are freshened the same as the thick, some parts must be either too salty or not salty enough. We are all becoming more concious of conserving natural resources and water is no exception, so if you use running water, it need not run very much. The salt is released slowly, and thick parts will take 24 hours or more.

If you use changes of water, change every few hours. The less frequently you change the water, the more time it takes to freshen.

Fish are freshened enough when there is not quite enough salt left to suit your taste (tasting is the only way I know to get salt just right). Remember that the fish will be dried during the smoking process, and salt will thus be concentrated.

Drain the freshened fish by placing the pieces on the smoking racks. (Commercial producers *waterhorse* the fish to squeeze more water out of them and reduce drying time in the smoker. They simply pile the pieces then weight the pile).

Now turn to instruction for Smoking Lox in this chapter.

HOW TO MAKE NOVA LOX
OR LOX SALMON

Kind of fish to use

Nova Lox can be made from fresh or frozen fish. I think frozen fish make a better product because some moisture is lost when the fish thaws. This seems to make it easier to get good slicing texture in the final product.

How to prepare the fish

If the fish are frozen whole, fillet them while they are still half frozen. This prevents the flesh from tearing during filleting. Follow normal filleting instruction in chapter 3.

I suggest that you also consider dividing the side into pieces according to thickness (see chapter 9). Lox is used thinly sliced at its best, so I use only the thickest, best slicing part of the fish for lox and the thinner part for kippering, drying, canning or eating fresh.

Dry salt-sugar mix for nova lox

a. **Make a mix** of 1 part brown sugar to 1 part pickling salt.
b. **Drysalt** by placing the pieces in a container of the salt-sugar mix. Scoop the mix over each piece; don't rub the mix in, but thoroughly cover it.
c. **Sprinkle some of the mix** on the bottom of a plastic or similar salt resistant container, pick each piece of fish up with as much of the mix as will adhere to it, and place it skin side down in the container.
d. **Sprinkle each layer** of pieces with salt-sugar mix, then add another layer, etc., placing the top layer skin side up. Leave the pieces in the salt-sugar mix as long as indicated in the following table.

Times in dry-salting mix

Thickness	Time
¾ in.	9 hrs.
1 in.	12 hrs.
1½ in.	18 hrs.
2 in.	24 hrs.

e. **Remove the pieces** from the dry-salt mix, rinse, and drain. Now brine the pieces in a 90° salinometer brine.

90° sal. brine

Pickling salt		Water
20 oz. (2½ cups)		64 oz.
	or	
630 g (630 ml)		2 l

f. **Crushed bayleaves may be added** to the brine.
g. **Cool the brine** and keep it cool (see chapter 8) while brining the fish according to this table.

Brining times

Thickness	Time
¾ in.	9 hrs.
1 in.	12 hrs.
1½ in.	18 hrs.
2 in.	24 hrs.

h. **Freshen the fish** after this brining. Use a *brisk* flow of fresh running water using the following table as a guide.

Freshening times

Thickness	Times
¾ in.	45 min.
1 in.	1 hr.
1½ in.	1½ hrs.
2 in.	2 hrs.

Use more or less time according to your taste.

i. **At this point decide** whether you want Nova Lox (smoked) or Lox Salmon (unsmoked).

j. **If your choice is Nova Lox** turn ahead to Smoking Lox instruction in this chapter.

k. **Lox Salmon** is the freshened fish that is *unsmoked;* it is dried just enough to firm it for slicing. Be sure not to heat the fish in drying, though. This will defeat the whole process which is designed to produce a sliceable product. A frost free refrigerator will dry and firm the fish sufficiently if it is left uncovered.

Lox Salmon will keep only about as long as fresh salmon, so use the product within a reasonable time.

SMOKING LOX

Smoking conditions are given for both Natural Draft and Forced Draft smokers (see chapter 7 under Smoking).

Smoking

	Forced-Draft	Natural-Draft
Smoke Temp.	85° F (30° C)	85° F (30° C)
Smoke Time	6 to 8 hrs.	12 to 16 hrs.
Smoke Density	Medium	Medium

a. **Smoke to get the color** you want (see Smoking chapter 8).

b. **Cool the fish** before wrapping. If even slightly warm fish (85° F) is wrapped it will sweat, then spoil in a short time.

c. **Freeze surplus fish** promptly. It has a limited refrigerator shelf life and any time spent before freezing will leave less shelf life after thawing.

Resume:

Old Fashioned Lox	Nova Lox	Lox Salmon
a. Freshen mild-cured fish	a. Apply dry-salt mix ·	a. Apply dry-salt mix
b. Smoke	b. Brine	b. Brine
c. Cool before wrapping	c. Freshen	c. Freshen
d. Freeze surplus promptly	d. Smoke	d. Dry
	e. Cool	
	f. Freeze	

SERVING LOX

LOX CORNUCOPIAS

Roll large slices of lox into cornucopias and secure shape with food pics. Fill with sour cream (flavored with horseradish if you like) or mashed hard cooked eggs bound together with softened cream cheese or sour cream.

LOX ROLLS

Spread slices of lox with cream cheese softened with a little milk or cream, then roll up. Overlap slices if necessary to get the size roll you wish. Use waxed paper to roll and to hold rolls together while they are refrigerated.

For serving slice the rolls and place the slices on crackers or toast rounds or squares.

LOX AND BAGELS

Directions for this delicacy seem superfluous, but here they are. Slice bagel in half cross-wise and toast lightly. Spread with cream cheese and top with slices of lox.

LOX OMELET

1 lb. lox 450 g	2 tbs. butter 30 ml
12 eggs	1 cup chopped onion 240 ml
16 oz. sour cream 450 ml	2 tbs. light cream 30 ml
6 oz. cream cheese 180 ml	

Mince *half* of the sliced lox and reserve the other half.

Fry the onions in the butter.

The recipe is for 2 omelets. Beat 6 eggs together with 1 tbs. (15 ml) of cream and pour into pan making sure to cover the bottom.

When the eggs have set, cover half of the pan with *half* of the sauteed onion and *half* of the *minced* lox and top with sour cream. Fold the plain half of the omelet over the filling and finish cooking.

Cook the second omelet and place them together on a warm serving platter, garnish the omelets with strips of the remaining lox.

Serve with sour cream, toasted bagels and cream cheese.

Serves 6.

Chapter **12**

Indian Smoked

Contents

Please read about Indian or Hard Smoked in chapter 6.

You will find that the low-fat salmon and trout make the longest keeping *Indian smoked* fish. The Indians long ago recognized that the oil in the fatter salmon, trout, and char made those dried fish go rancid. For example, the Native fishermen prized the low-fat *chum* salmon for drying. Indian smoked can be made from fresh fish, from frozen fish, and also from *hard salted* fish. I find that if I make *Indian smoked* from fat fish, it is best to keep it frozen or salted until I'm ready to eat it in a relatively short time. I do only as much at a time as can be used in two months, and I keep the dried fish refrigerated. My experience with fat, dried fish handled this way has been good. You will find that moderately *fat*, dried fish, cared for this way, can be taken out of the refrigerator and carried in your pack for at least a week before the fat begins to oxidize and acquire a slightly *off* taste. *Lean*, dried fish can be carried indefinitely as long as it's kept dry.

Freshening salted fish

I talk about salting salmon and trout in chapter 23, and also talk about the Hard salted fish being best used for smoking. Now let's talk about unsalting it so that it can be smoked. Before you can smoke the fish it must be freshened - nearly all the salt must be taken out. You can do the freshening in either running fresh water or in fresh water that is changed about every three hours. The total time it will take you will depend on three things:

(1) The thickness of the piece of fish. (2) Your individual taste for salt. (3) How long you have had the fish in the salt - the longer it has been in the brine the harder it is to get the salt out. The freshening time will be between 24 and 48 hours.

Taste for salt

There is no Freshening formula that I can give you for freshening. Only by tasting and gaining experience can you tell when the fish is fresh enough. One thing you must keep in mind in tasting for salt in this process - this fish will be *much drier* when it is done than any other smoked fish. This means that the salt in the fish when you put it in to dry, will be much more concentrated when it is finished drying. Other smoked products will contain from 50 to 75% moisture when finished, but *Indian smoked* should only have about 6%. You can readily see how much more the same beginning amount of salt will be concentrated in the drier product - about twice as much. If you can taste salt in the fish in the beginning, you can be sure it will be too salty when dried. This is another case where it is very important for you to keep records. If you record what you did and the result, you'll be much wiser the next time.

Commercial fish too salty

I am constantly finding that the commercial processes I have researched and tried, use too much salt. The commercial use of salt is understandable when you consider that more salt helps to get moisture released from the fish, thus cutting the amount that must be evaporated in the smokehouse. Also, extra salt is an insurance policy for the commercial producer in case the fish isn't thoroughly dried. With the extra salt it will still keep reasonably well. I keep working the salt down, trying to get a content of about ½%. This level gives good flavor and is apparently reasonable for normal, healthy people. Many commercial products contain in excess of 3% and some as much as 8%.

Native fish driers left the fish intact, with both fillets joined at the back and the backbone still attached at the tail. They then hung the fish to dry by draping the backbone over a pole.

You will probably find it more convenient in your smoker to dry either separate fillets or thin pieces of fillets left from fish whose thicker parts you processed by other methods.

The native originators of dried salmon used a sharp shellfish shell before knives were developed. Large mussel shells (as shown) were popular.

INDIAN SMOKED FROM FRESH OR FROZEN FISH

Salting Requires Care for the same reasons discussed under Freshening. The safest way to avoid too much salt, *is not to use any,* but some salt helps release moisture from the fish. You may also want some salt flavor in fish you dry for trail food. Keep in mind, however, that any salt will speed fat oxidation and rancidity. Here is my experience with reasonably fat fish (8 - 10% Fat). Cut for drying as illustrated.

90 ° Salinometer Brine

Pickling Salt	Water
10 oz. (1¼ cups)	64 oz.

or

300 g (300 ml)	2 L

Brining time in 90 ° Sal. Brine

Thickness	Time
2 in.	20 min.
1½ in.	15 min.
1 in.	10 min.
¾ in.	7 min.
½ in.	4 min.
¼ in.	2 min.

SMOKING DIRECTIONS FOR FRESH, FROZEN OR SALTED FISH

Temperature — 85° F - (38° C)
Time — *until thoroughly dry
Forced-draft — 30 hours
Natural-draft — to 3 weeks - depends on weather
Smoke — not too much - if smoked for whole drying period the smoke will likely be too strong

*The time honored test for dryness is when the fish or meat will snap like a *green* stick. The food must be cool otherwise it will not snap even if dry.

The finished product

Dried salmon and trout make an excellent trail food.

This nearly indistructable dried fish adds piquancy to soups and stews.

Hard smoked fish works well in many salted fish recipes. Here are some of the best:

Laksloda (Hydrate fish first)
Fritters with Skorthalia (Hydrate fish first)
Rougaille (Hydrate fish first)
Zapakanka
Raito (simmer unfreshened hard smoked with vegetables)
Al Accuiga (without anchovy - hydrate fish first)
Com Pimentos e Tomatoes (Cook fish in wine)
With Rice in a wine and Brandy Sauce, (hydrate first) See chapter 26 for recipes

Chapter 13

Smoking small trout

Please see chapter 6 for a discussion of smoked small trout and chapter 5 for methods of boning them for special presentation.

In chapter 9 you have seen that you may want to smoke small trout for 2 reasons: 1. Because they are delicious. 2. To change the taste of an otherwise inedible*muddy* or*grassy - tasting* fish.

Regardless of your reasons for smoking, you will go through the same smoking process except for 1 detail: fish that are smoked to cover an unpleasant taste will profit by your *scoring* the skin to let more smoke flavor in. Other normal tasting trout will also get more smoke flavor this way, but you may not want to mar their appearance for serving by breaking the skin.

Scoring the skin to let more smoke flavor in.

Smoking trout *unboned* vs. *boned*

Smoking trout unboned is certainly less trouble for you, the smoker, but a boned fish is certainly more interesting and appetizing to the eater. This is especially so when served to persons uninitiated in the fine art of eating a trout without getting a mouthfull of bones. It is my contention that people who say they do not like fish, don't dislike the flavor, it's the fear of getting a mouthful of bones that puts them off. At any rate, you may want to consider boning for special occasions.

If you decide to bone the fish you will have chosen one of the methods shown in chapter 5. Here is a list of all the ways that trout can be prepared for smoking.

Ways of preparing trout for smoking

a. **Unboned, as is,** just cleaned.
b. **Boning, Method 1.** Boned and cleaned through the back - belly left uncut.
c. **Boning, Method 2.** Boned and cleaned through the belly - back left uncut. Fish may simply be smoked boned, or it may be folded and the tail put out through the mouth (see chapter 5).
d. **Boning, Method 3.** Cleaned through the belly and boned through the back. Fish (as shown in chapter 5) can either be brined and smoked just boned - or the tail can be cut off and the fillets rolled.

In order to simplify this discussion of the various ways of doing small trout, I'll give directions for each method from brining, through smoking, on to suggestions for serving and hope it makes it more convenient for you that way.

UNBONED TROUT - BRINING - SMOKING - SERVING

Brine small trout in a 80° Sal. Brine

Pickling Salt	Water
17 oz. (2 1/8 cups)	32 oz.
or	
530 g (530 ml)	1 l

Cool the brine before using.

Brining time

Skin unscored	1½ hours
Skin scored	1 hour

Smoking

Please see chapter 7 for a discussion of different kinds of smokers.

To get unboned trout dried and smoked sufficiently, spit them through the eyes on a heavy wire (oiled, steel gas - welding rod or a light piece of dowling) and hold the belly open with small match - size sticks.

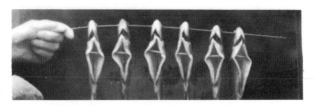

You hot smoke small trout because they are usually eaten cold. Smoke them in two steps for best appearance and texture: Step 1. Drying and smoking. Step 2. Cooking and smoking.

Smoking Schedule

	Forced-draft smoker	Natural-draft smoker
	Drying	
Smoke Temp.	90° F. (32° C)	90° F. (32° C)
Time	30 minutes	1 hr. or more - depends on weather
	Cooking	
Smoke Temp.	160° F. (77° C)	160° F. (77° C)
Time	1½ hours	3 hrs. or more - depends on weather

Cool fish before wrapping.

Smoked unboned small trout

Serving Suggestions

Served very simply, accompanied by sliced cucumber and lemon wedge, with a caper in the eye.

Served skinned, decorated with celery slice *scales* and pimiento in the eye.

Accompaniments consist of sliced tomato, sliced cucumber, sliced cooked beet, and hard cooked egg, dressed with green mayonnaise.

Serve chilled.

BONED TROUT - BRINING - SMOKING - SERVING

Boned trout, regardless of the method of boning, all take the same brining and smoking schedule.

Use a 80° salinometer brine (see formula under Brining Before Smoking - Unboned Trout).

Brining Time

8 minutes - stirring often.

~~~~~~~~

Hanging Smoked Trout for Smoking

I.   II.

I. Back boned (boning method 1) trout can be used as a *serving dish* for cold sliced vegetables. They must be *shaped* for this purpose prior to smoking. Spit them through the eyes with a heavy wire and shape the cavity with small match-size sticks.

II. Back boned and belly cleaned trout (boning method 3) will smoke best if suspended from a dowel.

III. Belly boned trout (boning method 2) smoke best suspended over a dowel. Use a metal skewer through the head and tail to hold the tail in place while smoking.

IV. Rolled boned trout (boning method 3) must be smoked rolled, sitting on a smoking tray.

Smoking boned trout

The smoking schedule for boned trout is the same as that for the un-boned ones - please see.

~~~~~~~~~~~

SERVING SUGGESTIONS FOR
BONED TROUT

The *boat - shaped* smoked fish (boning method 1) can be used as a serving dish for: sliced tomato, sliced, hard cooked egg, cooked beets, cucumber, etc., dressed with plain or green mayonnaise.

Serve chilled with lemon wedge, olive in the mouth and capers in the eyes.

The *folded* smoked trout (boning method 2) is shown with olive in mouth, capers in the eyes and decorative *sliced potato fish.* It is served accompanied by hard cooked egg quarters and quarters of cold beets and tomatoes, sliced cucumber and lemon wedge. Serve chilled with green mayonnaise.

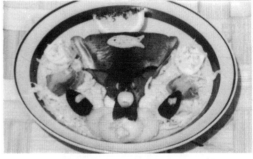

The open back and belly smoked trout (boning method 3) shown *stuffed* with sliced tomatoes, and garnished with parsley, lemon slices, hard cooked egg and caper in eye.

The same (boning method 3) smoked rolled trout shown as a base for cold egg and vegtable slices with olive in mouth and capers in eyes.

Chapter **14**

Making
pickle-smoked

Please read about Pickled - Smoked Salmon in chapter 6.

Getting ready to pickle

Prepare for the pickle-smoke cure by butchering as illustrated in chapter 4. As with other smoked salmon products, I suggest that you divide the fillet into pieces of different thickness (see chapter 9). By doing this, you can get both the thick and thin pieces pickled and smoked correctly.

Pickling procedure

This cure is similar to that used in corning meat. You use a flavored salt - sugar brine that is relatively weaker than the brines normally used for smoking. The fish stays in the brine for days, and acquires a *cured* taste like ham or corned beef.

Prepare the following

Pickle

4 qt.	water	4 l
1 lb. (2 cup)	brown sugar	480 g (480 ml)
1½ lb. (3 cup)	salt	720 g (720 ml)
1 oz. (4 tbs.)	mixed pickling spice	30 g (60 ml)

a. **Add fish pieces to the brine,** and keep it cool during the curing. This is a weak brine and the time in cure is long. It must be kept below 45° F

(7° C) - at refrigerator temperature is better.

b. **A *salinometer is useful*** in pickle curing if you are doing a large amount of fish and are serious about good quality. To get good curing, the salt content of the brine should stay at the proper level. The right level of salt allows the *curing* to proceed without undesirable bacteria spoiling the fish.

c. **Don't leave fish in pickle** that hasn't been kept up to 60° sal. for longer than the required time, because you may get what is known as *ropy* (stringy - drooling) brine. Ropy brine will spoil the flavor, so if you find this condition, wash the fish off carefully in fresh brine then cover it with fresh brine.

Since the fish will be taking salt out of the brine and putting water back in, you should check with a salinometer daily, then *dissolve* enough salt to bring the strength up to 60° sal.

If a small amount of fish is being pickled and you don't have a salinometer, use plenty of pickle in relation to fish - don't crowd the fish into a small amount of brine.

d. **Brining different thicknesses** requires a different technique in this process. Normally I put the thick pieces in first, then the thinner ones at appropriate intervals so they all come out together. In this long pickling process however, the thin pieces will be sitting in the refrigerator for days waiting their turn in the pickle. Under these circumstances, the thin pieces will keep fresher if they are pickled first. Put all pieces into the pickle at once, then take the thinner ones out after the required time. If the fish have been cut into pieces before freezing, it would certainly be better if you thawed the thick and thin pieces at different times - just before they are to go into the pickle. Alternately, you can smoke in two batches to prevent the thinner pieces from sitting around too long.

e. **Overhaul the pieces daily;** this is pickling parlance for moving them around so all get pickled evenly.

Pickling Times

Fillet Thickness	Fat Fish	Lean Fish
½ in.	30 hrs.	20 hrs.
¾ in.	40 hrs.	30 hrs.
1 in.	2½ days	40 hrs.
1¼ in.	3 days	2 days
1½ in.	3½ days	2½ days
1¾ in.	4 days	3 days
2 in.	5 days	3½ days
2½ in.	6 days	4¼ days
3 in.	7 days	5 days

f. **Rinse the pieces off** after the pickling and let surplus water drain off.

g. **Smoking is done cold** because the pickle cured fish is usually served thin sliced like Scotch smoked and Lox.

Smoking times given are for both natural draft and forced draft smokers (see Smoking, chapter 8).

Pickle-smoking schedule

Fillet Thickness	Forced-Draft smoker	Natural-Draft Smoker
thick	12 hrs.	up to 48 hrs.*
medium	10 hrs.	up to 40 hrs.*
thin	7 hrs.	up to 30 hrs.*
Temperature	Not above 85° F - 30° C	Not above 85° F
smoke	medium	medium

*Time in a natural draft smoker depends on the weather as discussed in Smoking - chapter 7. You will learn to feel when the fish is dried and firmed enough for slicing.

h. **Cool the finished product** down to near freezing as soon as possible after smoking. Do not wrap the fish in any way until it is thoroughly cooled. If you do wrap too soon, the fish will sweat and quickly spoil.

i. **Freeze any surplus fish** as soon as possible after cooling. Smoked fish has a refrigerator life not too much better than fresh fish. This life has a definite length, and if part of the life is used up before freezing, there will be that much less life left when the frozen fish is later thawed.

j. **Serve pickle-smoked** as you would Lox or Scotch Smoked.

Pickle-smoking is also the base for fish hams, see chapter 37

Chapter **15**

Making Seelachs

Please read about Seelachs in chapter 8 before starting this process.
Seelachs can be made from fresh, frozen, or salted fish.

In Germany, the birthplace of seelachs, commercial processors usually use salted fish, because they want to put the fish away at their prime for use all the rest of the year. Also the fish must be salted later in the process anyway, and since salting is cheaper than freezing, they salt them in the first place.

You, too, may find it useful or occasionally necessary to salt some white fish and want to make seelachs from them, so I'll describe the use of salted, as well as fresh or frozen fish.

The seelachs process

1. *Fillet the fish* for Seelachs, leaving the *skin on,* as usual; the skin helps protect the fillet during subsequent handling.
2. *For long keeping, salt* the fillets according to chapter 24 under *hard salting.*

For immediate use, drysalt the fillets. If they are thick score the skin to admit the salt. See chapter 8. In a salt-proof container place a *liberal* amount of salt on the fillets. Leave the fillets in the salt 24 hours to ensure the necessary firmness for handling during processing. Let the brine that forms run off.

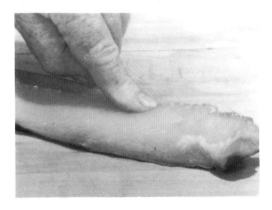

The fillets should feel firm and springy to the touch when salted enough.

5. **Freshening the Fish** before further processing is necessary whether they have been Hard - Salted or salted only enough for immediate use.

The commercial seelachs producer aims for a month or more of refrigerated shelf life. To help get this, he needs about 9% salt in the finished product. You, at home, needn't sacrifice good health and good flavor for shelf life, so you can freshen the fish until the salt taste is just right for you. Use running water or changes of water to remove the salt to taste. Keep in mind that the fish will dry during the smoking process, so the salt will be concentrated; consequently, freshen until there is less salt than you would normally want.

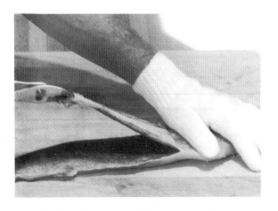

Now remove the skin that has been left on the fillet; pliers will help in this.

7. Slice the fish as thin as is practical, keeping in mind that you will have to handle the slices several times during dyeing, smoking, and packing. I can't tell you how thin to slice, because different species of fish have different muscle makeup; some species will stand thinner slicing than others. The amount of salt left in the fish will also affect firmness; the more salt the firmer the fish.

8. **Food Coloring** is used for dyeing the slices. I find this formula gives a good salmon color:

Water	150 ml or 5 oz.
5% vinegar	10 ml or 2 tsp.
Red food dye	30 drops
Yellow food dye	45 drops

Dyeing time will depend on the specie of fish and the slice thickness. Cut one of the thicker slices in half at 15 minutes to see dye penetration; 60 minutes is my longest dyeing time. Stir the slices in the dye to make sure they all get sufficient dye uptake.

9. **Drain the pieces** well so there aren't puddles of dye solution left to cause uneven coloring. The smoking trays are a good place for draining. *Make sure* that the trays are well oiled with *vegetable* oil so the slices won't stick.

10. **Smoking**

Temperature	85° F - 30° C
Time	30 to 60 minutes for Forced Draft Smoker
	1 to 2 hours Natural Draft Smoker
	according to taste

11. Pack the smoked slices in vegetable oil. The highest quality pack uses olive oil, but any edible oil will do.

12. Refrigerate the pack and keep it refrigerated for best shelf life. It will last up to a month depending on the amount of salt.

Chapter **16**

Smoking
for canning

Please read about Smoked Salmon for canning in chapter 6.

Because the fish is hot smoked in this process, and therefore inclined to crumble, you will find it easier to cut the side into can size pieces before it is smoked. The guide shown helps to get uniform pieces.

You can brine the thick and thin parts for the same time if you put some of each size into each can or jar. Use a 80° salinometer brine.

80° Sal Brine

Pickling salt	Water
40 oz. (5 cups)	4 qt.
or	
1260 g (1050 ml)	4 l

Brining time

Piece Thickness	Time
½ in.	10 min.
¾ in.	20 min.
1 in.	30 min.
1½ in.	40 min.
2 in.	1 hr.

Smoking

Smoking must be minimized to avoid harsh flavor in the finished product, but drying is just as important to quality. To get a balance between flavor and texture, it is necessary to smoke only part of the time, then continue drying. If you have a forced-draft smoker with supplementary heat, this is easy. But if your smoker is natural draft, there are two approaches you can use to solve the problem: 1. Use a small *clear* fire all the time to minimize the smoke, or 2. The surest way to control the amount of smoke is to smoke first, then continue drying in the kitchen oven. Use the lowest setting on the oven and leave the door ajar to lower the heat even further.

As explained in chapter 6, it is necessary for you to preheat your smoker. It should be at 110° F (44° C) when you put the fish in.

Smoking schedule

Forced-draft		Natural-draft
Temperature	110° F	(44° C)
Time	2½ hrs.	7 hrs. low smoke or 3½ hrs. then oven
Smoke density	medium	Depends on method chosen; as little as possible or medium if using oven.

Drying

Smoke	none	
Time	2 hrs.	2 hrs. in oven

Skinning the pieces is easiest when the fish is warm.

Pack the jars or cans as full as possible for two reasons: 1. unlike raw fish this is a *dry* pack - there will be little or no moisture in the can to conduct heat; air in the can is a poor conductor of heat. 2. your time is valuable and cans or jar lids are expensive. Get the most out of every container by filling it compactly.

It is impossible to properly fill containers unless you have some small strips to fit in. The thinner parts lend themselves better to cutting for this purpose, but cool them first and use a super-sharp knife to minimize crumbling.

Processing

Follow the instructions in chapter 35 To The Letter. Smoked fish improperly canned can be as deadly as any!

Chapter 17

Smoking roes and livers

Please see chapter 6 about Smoked Roes and Livers.

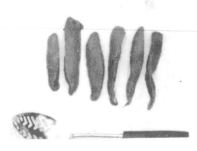

Roes that are immature are the best for smoking, since they are easier to use after processing.

Large, mature eggs rupture more readily.

PREPARING HARD ROES (FEMALE) FOR SMOKING

Fresh, frozen, or salted roes may be used for smoking.

1. **Salted hard roes** (see chapter 26) must be freshened in running water or changes of water up to 24 hours. Keep in mind that the roes will lose about 25% of their weight during smoking. This loss (moisture) will naturally concentrate any salt left in the roes after freshening.

Salting Fresh and Frozen hard roes

2. **Frozen roes** must be thoroughly thawed before salting for smoking; when thawed, salt them just as you would fresh roes.

3. **Fresh roes** may be brined or dry-salted. I prefer brining, and you may also, because it gives you an opportunity to add flavors to the roes if you wish. Flavors that are sometimes added in preparing commercial fish roes are: the various spices, brown sugar, or molasses. If you want added flavor see chapter 8 about flavored brines, otherwise use a plain 70° salinometer brine.

70 ° salinometer brine

Pickling salt	.	Water
16 oz. (2 cups)		64 oz.
	or	
500 g (500 ml)		2 l

4. **Brining times** for fresh or thawed hard roes range from 5 minutes for small roes to 30 minutes for 1 lb. (450 g) roes.

5. **Dry-salting times** for hard roes in dry pickling salt range from 30 minutes for small roes to 2 hours for 1 lb. (450 g) roes. After salting, roes must be thoroughly washed of salt.

6. **Drain roes** for 30 minutes after either being brined or after rinsing from dry salting.

Now turn to smoking hard and soft roes.

PREPARING SOFT ROES (MALE) FOR SMOKING

1. **Soft roes are just that - soft;** consequently, they benefit by some conditioning before smoking. Large soft roes (those around ½ lb. or 225 g each) need about 30 minutes in a 70° salinometer brine *before* conditioning. Small soft roes will be salty enough for smoking after the conditioning alone.

2. **Conditioning** consists of simmering them in salted water until they are firm enough to handle easily.

Raw soft roes left - Conditioned right

3. **Drain conditioned soft roes** well before smoking.

SMOKING HARD OR SOFT ROES

Be sure that screens on your smoking racks are well oiled before placing the roes. Both roes are cold smoked according to size.

Smoking

	Forced-draft smoker	Natural-draft smoker
Smoke Temp.	90° F (32° c)	90° F (32° C)
Time	2 to 6 hrs.	4 to 12 hrs.
	(according to size	(according to size and weather)
Smoke density	meduim	medium

SMOKING FISH LIVERS

Remove the gall bladder from the liver *carefully;* a broken gall bladder can mean a tainted liver. The safest way of removing it is, to slice off the portion of the liver to which the ball bladder is attached.

Livers need conditioning before smoking so they won't stick to the smoking trays. Condition them by dropping them into boiling salted water until they change color and get firmer. This will be enough salting before smoking for livers smaller than 4 oz. (112 g). Salt larger livers in a 70° sal. brine.

70 ° sal. brine

Pickling salt	Water
15 oz. (1 7/8 cup)	64 oz.
or	
460 g (460 ml)	2 l

Brine the livers according to weight

Wt. of liver	Time in brine
4 oz.	10 min.
8 oz.	30 min.
12 oz.	45 min.

Raw liver left - Conditioned right

Drain the brine from livers on the smoking trays. Livers are especially sticky, so make sure the trays are well oiled.

Smoking schedule

	Forced-draft smoker	Natural-draft smoker
Smoke	dense	dense
Temperature	90° F (32° C)	90° F (32° C)
Time	1 to 3 hrs.	2 to 5 hrs.
		depending on weather

Cool livers before wrapping.

USING SMOKED SOFT ROES

the soft roes may be chopped and creamed or chopped to serve in/or with scrambled eggs, or simply sautéed with or without eggs or bacon. But the French have a way with *Laitances*, the milk colored roe, or milt.

At any rate, if you are lucky while in France, you will be served the *milk* roe in fritter (en beignets) or in a sauce either en cassie (in tartlettes) or en canapé - (using toast for a *couch*).

MAKING FRITTERS (BEIGNETS)

Dice the smoked soft roes and marinate them in white wine, lemon juice, and finely chopped parsley while you make a fritter batter.

If you are making the fritters for the hors d'oeuvre use just a thickish batter. If, however, you are making them for an entrée, make a chou paste without flavoring or sugar.

Drain the marinade off the diced roe, and dry the dices by rolling around on paper towel.

Mix the roe into whichever fritter batter you choose and fry as any other fritter.

Serve with a cocktail sauce, or your favorite sauce.

CREAMED SOFT ROES

Marinate the diced soft roes as for fritters while you make a white sauce (Béchamel).

Drain the diced roes and add to the sauce. Thin if desired with cream and reheat for serving but do *not* boil!

Serve in tartelettes or on toast.

USING SMOKED HARD ROES

Smoked hard roes (female) can be used in making the cream salad, Taramosalata (see chapter 27) or in flavoring a number of sauces and dips made in a blender. They may also be used alone or with smoked liver to make a pate.

SMOKED ROE AND LIVER PATE

Here is a commercial recipe which you can spruce up by adding chopped onion, herbs, and spices usually used in pate.

½ lb. smoked hard roe 225 g
½ lb. smoked liver 225 g
2 tbs. potato starch 15 ml

Use a blender to chop the roe and liver. The membranes usually gather on the knives and separate themselves or can be separated by passing the paste through a strainer.

Mix in the starch and onions, herbs and spices if desired, and cook as directed for you favorite pate.

You can also make a pate from the smoked roes *without* liver.

SMOKED ROE PATE

| 1 lb. smoked hard roe 450 g | 4 tbs. potato starch 60 ml |
| 2 oz. pork fat 56 g | 1 tbs. tomato paste 15 ml |

You can also spruce up this commercial recipe by adding your own flavoring.

Use the blender on the roes as directed for liver and roe pate.
Put the fat through the finest plate of the meat chopper.
Mix all ingredients and cook as directed for you favorite pate.

USING SMOKED LIVERS

Smoked livers make an excellent pate. You can use any of numerous recipes to be found in cook books. I suggest, however, that you first try a recipe that calls for the liver to be diluted with 1/3 as much white veal as liver. With or without the veal you may want to include some bread crumbs and farina.

Chapter **18**

Smokers and smoking fuels

Have you ever wondered how fish smoking began? When I do, one scene I visualize is that of some early ancestor despairing because the dried fish, on which his life depends, spoils instead of drying during cool, damp weather. If he survived such a catastrophe, it probably didn't take him long to find that *fire* assured him of successful drying when weather turned bad.

From such a beginning, that ancestor gradually recognized that the smoke, incidental to the fire, also kept insects from eating the fish before he could. I'm sure that it was much later before that primitive fish *drier* began to enjoy the taste of smoke and became instead a fish *smoker*. And it probably took even longer for him to recognize that lengthy smoking also deposited something on fish that kept it from molding while it was stored. Certainly, fish smoking has come a long way since that simple beginning. I will trace the progress of the art from the beginning, to today's modern sophisticated smoking kilns, hoping that you find a smoker that best suits you.

The fireplace became a fish smoker

As man evolved and moved out of smoky caves, he still relied on fire for comfort. He did, however, find that the fire worked better if it had its own confined place - a fireplace. The chimney of the fireplace, thus became a natural place to get that smoky flavor for which he'd acquired a taste.

The railroad popularizes mild smoked fish

For a long time after the advent of the fireplace, people with access to fish, enjoyed them smoked. But with the coming of the railroad, which made possible speedier delivery of food, people far from the sea in such places as England, demanded a supply of the mild-smoked fish delicacies, too. Thus Fisherfolks enjoyed a ready market for the products of their smoky chimneys.

The fish smoking chimney moves outside

When faced with more orders than the home chimney could produce, rather then build a different, more efficient smoker, the new entrepreneurs simply built bigger chimneys without any houses attached. That way they needn't learn how to smoke all over again. In such a fashion, the growing industry continued to exist until World War II.

The revolution in fish smoking

Since the War a revolution has taken place in large scale fish smoking, but little such enlightenment has come to home smoking. For the serious home smoker and the small commercial smoked fish producer, I would like to tell why the commercial producers sparked this revolution, why they were dissatisfied with the *old fashioned* smokers, and what the home smoker can learn from them.

Why old smokers became inadequate

Critics of both the European and the American natural draft smokers agree that they were adequate for smoking in earlier times. Back then smoked fish products received days and even weeks in the smoker and the longer times allowed that curing be *averaged out*. In other words, it was less important that the smoke first went this way, then the other, or that some fish were dried ahead of the others. Over a long processing time they would eventually all get smoked enough and dried enough.

When smoked fish consumers began demanding more mildly cured fish, that were processed for hours rather than days or weeks, the inadequacies of the natural draft smokers were all too apparent. In commercial production, it has taken a long time for the older smokers to be replaced by forced draft, controlled ones because the short-comings of the equipment has been compensated for by the skill of the operators. One thing that has made a change necessary in recent years is the shortage of skilled workers. The work is so unattractive, that few are inclined to learn the art anymore.

Workers had to climb around in the smoky chimneys shifting fish many times, to compensate for the capricious wandering of the smoke. Sometimes all the fish had to be moved several times. A final piece of tedium came after fish were smoked; then they often had to be hand washed to remove ash that blew up from the fires. In almost every batch of fish some of the lower ones were lost by getting too hot, cooking, then falling into the fire.

Specific shortcomings of older smokers

You have seen in chapter 10, that for most processes it is desirable to control smoke temperature - to keep it below 30° C for cold smoking, and, when hot smoking, to be able to raise it in controlled amounts. With fires built on the floor of the smoker, control is difficult. Often a sudden change in the draft will blow the fire up and overheat the fish. Heat control is so much of a problem in natural draft smokers that often several small fires are built in an effort to better control it. Scandinavian sardine smokers build the fires on wagons so that they can be moved about in an effort to better control temperature. Temperature recorders set in natural draft smokers show that in spite of every effort to keep smoke below 30° C it will at times rise in bursts to as much as 60° C - 140° F instead of staying at the desired 85° F.

Most products require a definite amount of dehydration during the smoking process to improve keeping, to change texture, or to improve the pack if the product is to be canned. Dehydration in the case of cold smoking, must be done by the smoke. In natural draft smokers that is first of all a problem in getting a draft going at times. For there to be a draft the smoke must rise up through the smoker. For this to happen the smoke must be warmer than the outside air. If the outside air approaches the smoking temperature limit of 30° C, then it cannot be heated and there can be no draft. Often under conditions like these there is a slight temperature differential and a slight draft, but the air is saturated enough with moisture so that there is no drying. Even with an adequate draft, the design of older smokers is such that the smoke will take the path of least resistance or will wander about making the smoking and drying uneven. It is usually the case with these smokers that the smoke picks up moisture from the lower fish in the smoker and is saturated by the time it gets to the upper ones. In this case every rack of fish has a different rate of drying and much shifting of racks becomes necessary.

Another product of the draft problems is getting adequate smoking. If there is no draft, there is no smoking going on - smoking, drying, everything comes to a standstill. If the product is a lightly salted one - as all our mildly cured fish are - it will spoil under these conditions. Everything is ideal for spoilage; warm, moist air around warm, moist fish - no drying or smoke deposition going on. The fish will either have to be removed and put back under refrigeration or be lost. What then has been done to alleviate these problems?

How modern smokers overcome smoking problems

Forced draft smokers have been designed to overcome each of the problems encountered with the older *natural* draft ones. they have come from most of the countries that have any fish smoking industry. Technologists in these countries all recognized the problems of their industries, and worked toward solving them. Some designs differ quite a bit from others, but they all accomplish the same thing - they *control the smoking process.*

Instead of relying on the smoke in the smoker to rise by being warmer than the outside air, the modern smoker makes a draft by means of a fan or blower. By mechanically moving the air instead of waiting and praying that it will move by itself, the wastefulness of the old smokers is eliminated also. Much of the time, the old natural drafters wasted a lot of heat and smoke, because they had to be exhausted to get draft. Anyone knows how expensive heat is, and not to be easily dismissed either is the cost of smoke-making material. Instead of smoke passing through once as before, the forced draft permits *recirculation.* Now, if the air is not too saturated to do more drying it is recirculated and the smoke given another chance to deposit on the fish. In practice, what really happens is that some of the smoke is exhausted from the smoker constantly, and some new smoke and some new dry air comes in to take its place. This way the maximum

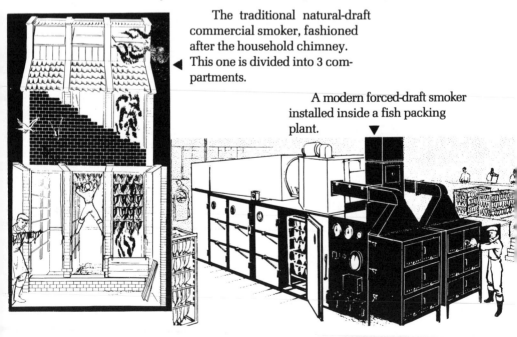

The traditional natural-draft commercial smoker, fashioned after the household chimney. ◄ This one is divided into 3 compartments.

A modern forced-draft smoker installed inside a fish packing plant. ▼

amount of drying and the desired amount of smoking is constant. Should the air coming in be too warm and/or too wet, it is cooled by running it over a tray of ice or over cooling coils. The moisture will condense out on the ice or the coils just like moist kitchen air does on the cool window. This cool low-moisture air is now heated by the heaters in the smoker, and in being heated will expand and be quite dry. To better explain, if a unit of incoming air contains 40% water vapor and is heated and expands to two units of air, it then only contains 20% water vapor. It is a much better drying medium as a result.

Smoke quality improved

The quality of the smoke can be pretty much controlled by how the smoke material is burned. (see smoking fuels). If combustion is at the right level the smoke is made up largely of almost invisible particles - which give the finest smoke flavor. In the forced draft smoker, the positive draft is used to pull a controlled amount of combustion air through a remote smoke producer, then draw the smoke into the smoker. There is, therefore, a fine degree of control possible where virtually none was available in the older smokers.

Why didn't modern smoker appear earlier

You may wonder why forced draft smokers were not designed much earlier. Probably many thought about it and even tried it, but it isn't all that simple. To get air circulation is not enough. The old problem of air taking the path of least resistance does not go away just because a fan is installed. It gets even worse because of the increased velocity. The new smoker must be designed so that the smoke is divided up and evened out in order that all the fish get an even amount. The engineering for doing this has been around for quite a while, but for some reason engineers and the commercial fish smoking people didn't get together.

In almost all cases technicians from government research institutions saw the need for change and dug out the necessary know how.

Forced draft smoker results

The superiority of the forced draft smoker over the older natural draft one is not a matter of speculation on my part. It is the result of about five years of using my own forced draft model. But in the event that I might seem prejudiced, here is a report on the subject by the Pacific Fisheries Experimental Station of the Fisheries Research Board of Canada.

"The purpose of this report is to point out the reduction in smoking time which may be obtained using an air conditioned kiln which makes possible a higher turnover rate per cubic foot of space, and a better quality, more uniform product. In addition, positive control of temperature and humidity, ease of operation and elimination of waste through fly ash, dropped fish and oversmoking, are valuable features."

"An air conditioned tunnel operating on the principle of circulating the fish was constructed at this Station some three years ago to carry out investigation on both smoking and dehydration of fish. Since then it has been used successfully in producing a great many types of commercial smoked fish products. A comparison of the time required to smoke these products with the average time taken in commercial kilns is shown in the accompanying table."

Average time in hours

Variety	Commercial Smokehouse	Air-conditioned Smoker
Salmon (smoked	12 - 15	5
Salmon (hardsmoked)	48	10 - 12
Salmon (kippered)	7 - 13	3 - 6

I have found the shortened smoking time in my *forced draft* smoker, very important when smoking during warm weather. I can do the entire job during the cool time of the day, whereas with *conventional* equipment there would be no hope. It would take the cooler part of a number of days.

What conclusions for the home smoker?

So much for describing the old and the new in commercial smoker, and talking about their advantages and disadvantages. You now know what it takes to do a good job of making barbecued, hot, and cold smoked products. You can see the difficulties in trying to produce the refined products in the older smokers and the relative ease with which they can be make in more modern smokers. Now, how does all this apply to the home smoker; what does it mean to him? Not too much I'm afraid unless you are willing to build your own smoker. Most amateur smokers will be satisfied to accept the ready availability and the ease of operating the *store bought* small smoke cookers, and pass on doing anything more refined than they allow.

Other, somewhat more serious smokers, can probably find something to suit their purpose in the traditional smokers, that have been around for most of this century, which I will show. For those who are most determined, those who wish to do a wide assortment of smoked goods and do them well, I'll show some forced-draft smokers so you can contemplate building your own, as I have done.

Understand smoking equipment limitations

It is important that the home smoker understand that he can't make all the traditional smoked products from trout and salmon is just any kind of a "smoker." I remember a man, who, after having asked me for smoking advice, said, that he was going to make lox in his covered barbecue. "It would be wonderful for the job," he said "Because it made *steam* and would make it nice and moist." His was probably a wonderful smoke cooker, but not suited for making lox. All I could do was say, "Good luck!" He wasn't interested in hearing that his wonderful cooker couldn't work magic.

Not too long ago, I read in a book on smoking, that the home smoker should buy an electric slicer if he wanted to turn out the slices salmon like you buy in a delicatessen. All the slicers in the world won't help unless the fish has been processed *properly* in smoking equipment capable of turning out that kind of product. Again, don't expect to work *miracles* by sheer force and determination. Either be satisfied to enjoy products that are within the limitations of your equipment, or acquire equipment that will do the job. It doesn't have to be complicated equipment; simple equipment will work. It just requires more care and expertise from you.

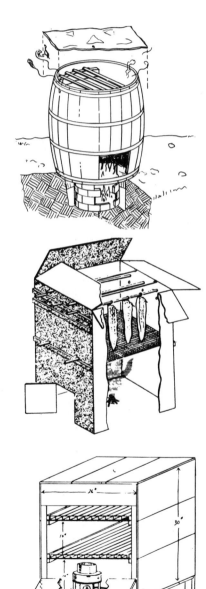

The simplest form of fish smoker - a topless and bottomless barrel over a smokey fire in a hole in the ground. The barrel has a cover of metal, wood, or canvas.

Barrels are a little difficult to come by these days. A cardboard box is more available now.

A simple, but slightly more sophisticated smoker is a custom built box with an electric hotplate which furnishes heat and ignites sawdust or chips in a pan.

The simple fish and smoke holder connected with a remote smokey fire by means of a covered pipe or earth covered ditch. The remoteness of the fire makes cold smoking possible.

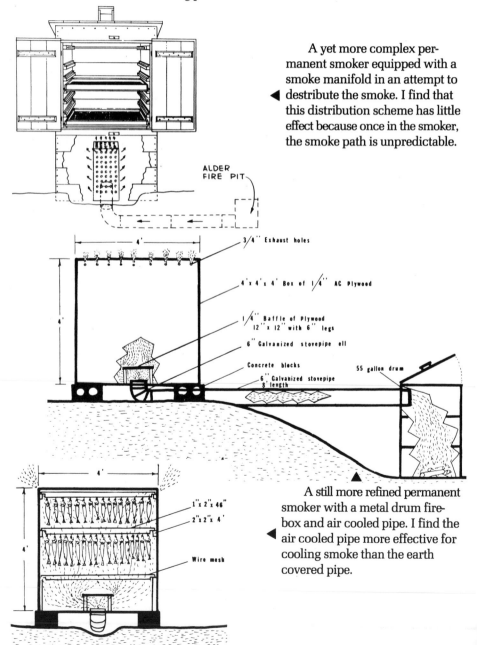

A yet more complex permanent smoker equipped with a smoke manifold in an attempt to destribute the smoke. I find that this distribution scheme has little effect because once in the smoker, the smoke path is unpredictable.

ALDER FIRE PIT

3/4″ Exhaust holes

4′ x 4′ x 4′ Box of 1/4″ AC Plywood

1/4″ Baffle of Plywood 12″ x 12″ with 6″ legs

6″ Galvanized stovepipe ell

Concrete blocks

6″ Galvanized stovepipe 8′ length

55 gallon drum

A still more refined permanent smoker with a metal drum firebox and air cooled pipe. I find the air cooled pipe more effective for cooling smoke than the earth covered pipe.

1″ x 2″ x 46″

2″ x 2″ x 4′

Wire mesh

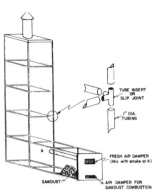

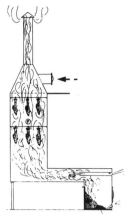

An idea for a portable smoker that can be slipped apart for carrying. The frame can be fitted with a canvas cover. The fresh air damper allows mixing cool air with the warm smoke in an attempt to control smoke temperature.

A similar design, made of knockdown sections of sheet metal. This design offers a crude method of converting the normally natural-draft smoker to a forced draft by attaching a suction fan at the smoke vent

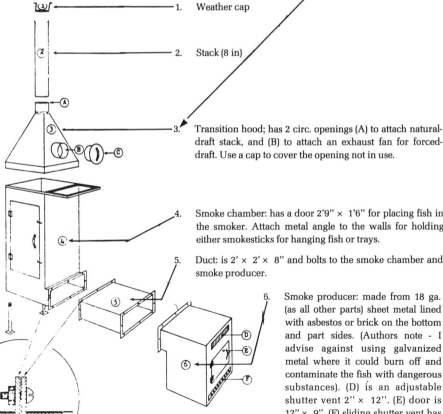

1. Weather cap

2. Stack (8 in)

3. Transition hood; has 2 circ. openings (A) to attach natural-draft stack, and (B) to attach an exhaust fan for forced-draft. Use a cap to cover the opening not in use.

4. Smoke chamber: has a door 2'9" × 1'6" for placing fish in the smoker. Attach metal angle to the walls for holding either smokesticks for hanging fish or trays.

5. Duct: is 2' × 2' × 8" and bolts to the smoke chamber and smoke producer.

6. Smoke producer: made from 18 ga. (as all other parts) sheet metal lined with asbestos or brick on the bottom and part sides. (Authors note - I advise against using galvanized metal where it could burn off and contaminate the fish with dangerous substances). (D) is an adjustable shutter vent 2" × 12". (E) door is 12" × 9". (F) sliding shutter vent has nine 1 inch holes cut in the sheet metal. A metal slide strip is held in place by runners attached to the sheet metal.

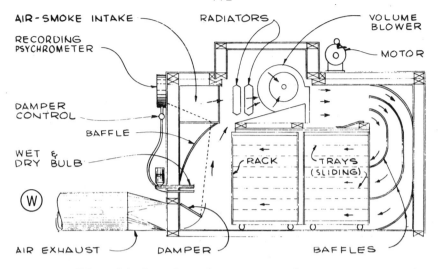

AIR-SMOKE INTAKE — RADIATORS, VOLUME BLOWER

RECORDING PSYCHROMETER — MOTOR

DAMPER CONTROL

BAFFLE

WET & DRY BULB — RACK — TRAYS (SLIDING)

(W)

AIR EXHAUST — DAMPER — BAFFLES

A small forced draft smoker utilizing some modern air engineering. The smoke generator is remote allowing smoke cooling. Fresh cool air can be mixed with smoke. Smoke can be selectively recirculated and/or exhausted. The circulating air-smoke mix can be heated to any desired temperature. The humidity of the incoming air can be controlled by passing it over cooling coils or a bed of ice.

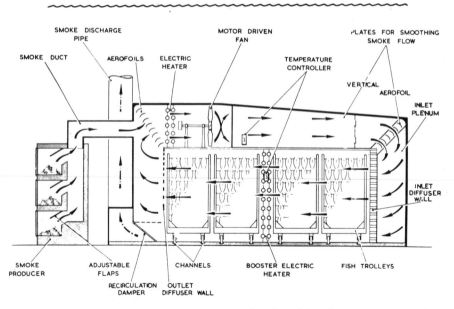

SMOKE DISCHARGE PIPE — MOTOR DRIVEN FAN — PLATES FOR SMOOTHING SMOKE FLOW

SMOKE DUCT — AEROFOILS — ELECTRIC HEATER — TEMPERATURE CONTROLLER

VERTICAL AEROFOIL

INLET PLENUM

INLET DIFFUSER WALL

SMOKE PRODUCER — ADJUSTABLE FLAPS — CHANNELS — BOOSTER ELECTRIC HEATER — FISH TROLLEYS

RECIRCULATION DAMPER — OUTLET DIFFUSER WALL

A cut away view of the Torry kiln developed by the Torry Research Laboratory, Aberdeen, Scotland. From an air engineering standpoint, I consider this design to be one of the best.

My present forced-draft smoker is much the worse for wear, having been out in the weather for 9 years. After much experimentation and redesign it's pretty foolproof now.

SMOKING FUEL

When discussing food smoking with a group, you can almost depend on a lively argument over *which is the best wood for smoking.* If the group is large enough, you will find proponents for almost any wood grown, as well as for peat, corncobs, rice hulls, fruit pits, and even, in desperation, dried animal dropping. One general rule I have learned about the suitability of fuel for smoking, is, "Don't ever generalize"; I'll try to explain why.

Coniferous woods bad for smoking?

In 40 years of fish smoking and researching the subject, I have read one general admonition hundreds of times: "Most any wood is suitable, except *coniferous;* it imparts a *pitchy* flavor." Then in recent years I have found technical reports from various countries contradicting that *sage* advice; for example:

Some of the most famous brands of Scotch smoked salmon use *juniper* along with oak.

Polish fish smoking technologists found that pine was equal to the hardwoods for smoking herring, and best of all for sprats (sardines).

One posh resturant in a large Canadian city is famous for its own *house smoked* salmon. I learned that its secret for success was smoking with fir!

Canadian fisheries technologists found that hemlock sawdust, along with green juniper twigs, gave a good smoked product with chum salmon.

Which wood for which fish?

German food scientists, after much research on food smoking, have reached a similar conclusion to mine: "Don't genealize about smoking fuels." The German scientists concluded that apparently the smoke flavors absorbed by the food vary according to both the *nature* of the food, and the *source* of the smoke. In other words, different foods (and different fish) will have different flavors when smoked with the same wood.

So the general admonition against using coniferous woods may be right for smoking lean fish (which includes most of the species), but *may* be wrong for fat fish. I use green juniper twigs under oak sawdust, and find the resulting cold smoked salmon well liked.

Sauce for the goose but not for the gander

Another reason for keeping an open mind about smoking fuels is shown in the results of a very scientifically conducted experiment by the Fisheries Research Board of Canada.

The researchers tested 12 different woods, used for smoking whitefish, under identical conditions. The smoked fish were then scored by taste panels who found the various products ranging from good to distasteful. One of the outstanding results, in my opinion, was the finding that hard maple and hickory - both famous for smoking hams and bacons - were marginal in acceptability for smoking whitefish. Another eyeopener for me was the result of using 3 different kinds of oak. I had always felt that oak was oak - one as good as another. Not so in this test; red oak was found good, white oak fair, and burr oak distasteful.

I conclude that each of you must try your different woods with your local fish. *But* after years of experimentation with various smoking fuels, I also must agree with the scientists of the Washington State Department of Fisheries when they talk about the *quality* of smoke - and that's a whole new subject - Smoke Generation (smoke making).

SMOKE MAKING

The way you make the smoke has a definite effect on the flavor it gives food. As discussed in *Smoke Quality Improved,* there are two kinds of smoke particles - large and small. The large (very visable) particles tend to be *tarry;* they give the more *undesirable,* creosotey flavor to food. The small, less visable (often nearly invisible) smoke particles are the more *desirable* ones; they tend to give a subtle, pleasant flavor to food.

Rate of burning controls smoke quality

The rate at which the smoke fuel burns controls the quality of smoke. Of course the rate of burning depends on two variables: 1. Dryness of the wood. 2. Amount of oxygen available.

It is easier to control smoke quality if the variables are reduced to one - the amount of oxygen available - so, use dry fuel.

Control of oxygen is much simpler if you use sawdust instead of wood. With sawdust, your fuel has a consistant composition; with wood the composition is always varying. Pieces of wood are made up of several layers, many of the layers vary from those next to them - some burn better than others. Pieces of wood will smoulder along, putting out a given amount of heat and smoke, until finally all of the volatile elements are gone, then the piece suddenly becomes a mass of white - hot coals. Zoom! Up goes the temperature - out of control! Sawdust on the other hand is a well mixed aggregate of all the layers of the wood. Each small particle does not go through a complicated series of combustion processes as a complex piece of wood does. The minute piece of sawdust is consumed in a second, thus the smoke making process becomes a series of small *puffs* of combustion each like the one before, and the one after. Feed the pile of dust a *given* amount of oxygen and it will put out a *given quality* of smoke.

MORE FIRES FOR MORE SMOKE

The easiest way to control *quantity* of smoke is to use more than one fire. Multiple fires give the commercial operator the options of light, medium, and dense smoke, because different products demand different amounts of smoke.

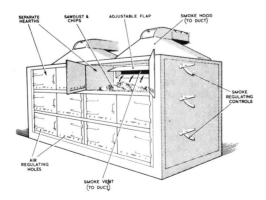

3
MARINATING

CONTENTS

Chapter **19**

About marinades

Whether you call it Marinade, Escabechar, Einpolken, Lagga in Lag, Seviche, or Pickle, they all mean the same in different parts of the world - *very* tasty pickled fish.

North Americans, in general, don't know about the good taste of pickled fish. But after being initiated, they are like epicures around the world, they *enjoy*. If you will try some of these recipes, it's likely that you too will become a marinade fan, because salmon and trout make some of the tastiest fish marinades.

Why call them marinades

I choose to call these products marinades rather than pickles for two reasons: (1) Most North Americans immediately think of a pickle as a preserved cucumber. (2) The word *pickle* in the fish trade, means the brine that forms when fish are salted. Furthermore, marinade is the usual English term for these products (in the Old World where they originated).

Background of marinades

Marinades are age-old delicacies, developed primarily as a means of preservation rather than a taste delight. They were needed for survival!

Before marinading was discovered, salt was widely used for preservation, but fish that is salted enough to be preserved is far too salty to eat, and is hard and tough to the point that it must first be conditioned for use. In short, it took considerable time and planning, and lots of precious drinking water for freshening before the salt fish could be eaten.

The inconvenience of salted fish was dramatically overcome with the discovery that alcoholic beverages, which had gone bad and turned to vinegar, would preserve fish. The early discoverers neither knew nor cared that the acid in the vinegar prevented food spoilage organisms from growing. They only knew that the fish didn't go bad and was always available for eating without any planning, waiting, or preparation. All the processing could be done when the fish were caught; from then on they were ready to eat.

Marinading is best known now for improving taste

Although marinading is still a very useful process that enables the sport fisherman to preserve his catch under certain conditions (lack of freezing facilities, far from home, etc.), it is now best liked for the new flavors it gives to fish.

The new flavors are a result of gradual changes that happen while the vinegar and salt keep the fish from spoiling. Experts say, "There is a ripening". It is a change similar to the ripening of cheese, or the curing of ham, bacon, or corned meats. Many enjoy marinated fish more because of the flavor change. They claim, "It doesn't taste like fish anymore".

Food acids other than vinegar will preserve also

I have used the word vinegar so far, rather than use the sometimes frightening term *acid*. But it is the *acid* in the vinegar that does the work of preserving. Other food acids will work just as well. Citrus juice, or dry white wine will work alone or in conjunction with vinegar.

Salt is also a necessary ingredient in marinading

If vinegar or other sources of acid were used alone to preserve fish, the fish would soon turn too soft to be enjoyed. Just as too much salt, in the case of salted fish, made the fish tough, just enough salt with the acid will keep the fish from becoming too soft. This is what marinading is all about - balancing the acid and salt to get preservation with just the right texture for eating.

Spices soften the bite of vinegar

The amount of vinegar necessary for preservation may be too strong for many palates. By adding spices you can soften the bite, and add to the overall enjoyment of the marinade. Sugar or other sweetener may also be added to soften the vinegar. Vegetables too can be used to dress *up* the appearance of the pack, to soften the vinegar's bite, and to add to the overall good flavor.

There are three different classes of marinades

1. COLD MARINADES are made from raw fish, but the acid changes the texture of the fish to a cooked-like condition.
2. COOKED MARINADES are made from fish that you poach or simmer in an acidic broth. You then preserve it in an acidic broth, jelly, or sauce.
3. FRIED MARINADES are either pan or deep fried fish preserved in an acidic broth or a sauce.

Chapter **20**

Cold
marinades

There are a number of cold marinades. They vary from those you keep overnight before eating, to those that are kept for more than six months. I will separate them into:

(a) Short-keeping cold marinades
(b) Medium-keeping cold marinades
(c) Long-keeping cold marinades

SHORT KEEPING COLD MARINADES - SEVICHES

Perhaps the most famous of the short keeping cold marinades is Seviche or Cebiche (depending on what part of Latin America the recipe comes from). Lemons or limes usually furnish the acid for these Latin preparations, with occasional help from dry wine, or wine vinegar.

These marinades originated before the days of refrigeration, when the only way to keep fish in the warmth of Latin America, was to marinate it in acid sauce of some kind. Now with refrigeration available in most places, the *good taste* of the seviche is still an excellent reason for using the old recipes. As a matter of fact, the old recipes are even better today when you are able to make the marinade more inviting and refreshing by chilling it before serving.

How to make a tangy ceviche

2 lbs. boned fillets (.9 kg)	1 cup wine vinegar (250 ml)
salt	2 hot chilis
freshly ground pepper	1 cup white wine (250 ml)
2 large onions	1 cup lemon juice (250 ml)

Optional seasonings

¼ tsp. oregano (1.5 ml)	½ tsp. cilantro (3 ml)
1 tsp. chili powder (6 ml)	2 oz. olive oil (60 ml)

Optional accompaniments

sweet potatoes, cooked, sliced	sweet corn, 2½ in. pieces
fresh tomato wedges	sweet pepper rings
hard cooked eggs	sour cream

1. **Prepare the fish** by filleting and boning (see chapters 3&4).

   If the fillets are thin, cut them into strips; if thick cut into bite size pieces.

2. **Season** by placing fish in a glass or ceramic bowl and sprinkling with 1 tsp. salt (6 ml) and 1 tsp. pepper.

3. **Marinate** by covering the seasoned fish with the wine and lemon juice.

4. **Prepare onions;** slice thinly, soak them in 1 tsp. salt in 1 cup water for 15 minutes. Rinse them then soak in the vinegar for 1 hour.

5. **Prepare the chilis** by removing the seeds and membrane, and either mincing or slicing thinly.

6. **Combine the ingredients** at least 2 hours before serving: Add onions and peppers to the fish, sprinkle with any or all of the optional seasonings. Add the optional sour cream, if desired, carefully toss, and *refrigerate* for at least 2 hours before serving.

WARNING

There are recent medical reports of humans being infected with parasites from eating raw fish in several forms, one of these being seviche. The acid treatment in seviche DOES NOT KILL SUCH PARASITES, only freezing or cooking will. Consequently, only use fish that has been frozen for seviche, it still makes an excellent cold dish.

MAKING A FANCY SEVICHE

2 lbs. (1 kg) boned fillets	1 cup scallions (250 ml)
salt	3 cloves minced garlic
5 parts lime juice*	1 tsp. fr. gr. pepper (6 ml)
1 part white wine vinegar*	1 tsp. sugar (6 ml)
3 hard cooked eggs	1½ tsp. mustard (6 ml)
1½ cups fresh tomatoes (375 ml)	1 cup salad oil (250 ml)
3 tbs. parsley (50 ml)	1 cup coconut cream (250 ml)†
½ cup celery (125 ml)	

* make sufficient quantity of marinade in these proportions to cover fish.

† to make coconut cream, cut fresh coconut into small pieces, blend in hot milk, and strain off solids.

PREPARE THE FISH by filleting and boning (see chapter four under CARING FOR THE CATCH AND BUTCHERING FISH). If the fillets are thin, cut them into strips; if thick, cut into bite size pieces.

1. **Marinate the fish,** in a glass or ceramic bowl, with enough of the lime juice-white wine mixture to cover. Sprinkle with 1 tsp. salt and let stand for 6 hours at *room temperature.*

2. **Combine the vegetables,** seasonings, salad oil, and coconut cream, and let stand while fish is marinating; keep this mixture cool.

3. **Add fish** to the vegetable mixture, toss carefully, and *refrigerate overnight.*

4. **Serve** on lettuce after draining, and garnish with any of the optional accompaniments given with the **tangy seviche.**

HOW TO MAKE A MEDIUM LONG-KEEPING COLD MARINADE

Here is a recipe for keeping fish one to two months. You can use either salted or fresh fish. I find that some fish are too fat or too watery to be enjoyed fresh. Often such fish can be improved by mild salting (see chapter 24). The salting firms the fish, which then makes a good marinade.

1. **If using salted fish,** freshen for at least 24 hours in running water or a number of changes of fresh water, until the salt tastes right.

2. **Cut the fillets** into either bite or serving size pieces depending on whether you want to serve it for the hors d'ouvre, luncheon or fish course.

3. **Place the fish** in a glass or ceramic container

For 2 lbs. or 1 kg of fish

Simmer together for 30 minutes

1 cup vinegar 5% (260 ml)	1 medium onion, sliced
1 cup water (260 ml)	1 lemon, sliced
1 tsp. salt (6 ml)	1 tbs. mixed pickling spices (18 ml)
3 tsp. sugar (18 ml)	1 clove mashed garlic

4. **Cool the mixture.**

5. **Pour the mixture over the fish** pieces and refrigerate for at least 24 hours before eating. The marinade will be better if left several days before using.

LONG-KEEPING COLD MARINADES

A distinctive flavor distinguishes these marinades from the *quickies* that have been described previously. Such a fine flavor can only be developed with time and with precise control of the preserving acid and salt. The use of spices and vegetable garnishes certainly adds to the flavor, but the most distinctive flavor comes from enzymes digesting the fish protein into simpler compounds. It is these new compounds that give the wonderful flavor.

In order to preserve the fish long enough for the desired change to take place, you go through two steps: 1. Treat the fish in a vinegar-salt brine called the *pickling* brine; this preserves it. 2. When the fish is completely penetrated by the *pickling* brine, put it in either a weaker *finishing* brine, or in a covering sauce. In this second phase, most of the desired change occurs.

These marinades also important for preserving

This process not only gives fish superior flavor, but is important as a means of preserving. If the weather is cool, or refrigeration is available, fish can be kept in the pickling bath (step 1) for up to 6 months before being finished for eating. Fish preserved this way can also be transported more simply than frozen fish, and with a minimum of ice.

MAKING LONG-KEEPING COLD MARINADES

Step 1

| fresh or salted fillets | vinegar 5% strength |
| or whole small fish | pickling salt |

Freshen salted fillets or whole small fish up to 24 hours in running water, or frequent changes of water, until the salt is removed to taste.

Cut the fresh or freshened fillets into small enough pieces for easy penetration of the pickling brine. Whole small fish, if fat, will brine faster if they are opened along the back.

Drain the fish thoroughly after freshening or washing so that excess water won't dilute the pickling brine that comes next.

The pickling brine is critical. There must be enough brine, and it must be strong enough to accept water coming out of the fish (which may be up to 80% of the fish's weight) without becoming too dilute to preserve the fish. To get the right ratio, *weigh the fish.*

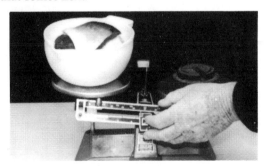

Prepare brine as follows

Fish	5% Vinegar	Pickling salt
3 parts	2.2 parts	0.2 parts
	example	
3 lbs.	32 oz. liq.	3.5 oz.
3 kg.	2.08 l.	200 g.

One liquid oz. of salt happens to weigh one oz., and one ml. of dry salt weighs one g.

Containers for the pickling brine must be vinegar and salt proof, i.e. of stainless steel, plastic, glass, ceramic, or wood.

Brining fish must be started right; the fish cannot simply be dumped into the brine; the pieces must not be allowed to stick together. The pieces should be stirred frequently the first day, and will cure faster and more evenly if stirred daily until cured.

Curing time at the ideal curing temperature of 50 to 55° F (10 to 12° C) is 10 to 15 days, depending on the thickness of the pieces. You can cure at other temperatures; at room temperature curing can take as little as 3 days, and below 50° F may take more than 3 weeks. If in doubt, leave it longer - but *not* much longer at *room temperature*.

Remember, however, that if necessary or convenient this cured fish can be kept up to 6 months in the refrigerator.

Rinse the fish off coming out of the brine when you are ready for step 2 - packing in the finishing brine.

Step 2

Read over the following FINISHING METHODS, and choose the one that appeals to you.

Choice of finishing methods

1. Plain vinegar-salt brine.
2. Vinegar-salt brine with spices.
3. Vinegar-salt brine with vegetable garnishes and spices.
4. Covering sauce.

Step 2, Method 1 - Plain vinegar-salt brine

For finishing brine, use the pickling brine that the fish came out of in step 1, it will give the best flavor, as long as its appearance does not put you off. Dilute it with an equal amount of water to make the finishing brine.

Fresh finishing brine can also be made if you wish, here are the proportions;

Finishing brine

Vinegar 5%	Water	Pickling Salt
1.5 part	3.5 parts	2 %
	example	
30 oz.	70 oz.	*20 oz.
30 ml	700 ml	*20 g.

*salt may be measured or weighed because wt. equals measure.

Pack the fish preserved as in step 1, into vinegar and salt proof containers (glass, ceramic, or plastic).

Cover the fish with the *finishing* brine, being sure to exclude any air that may be trapped. Be sure that all pieces are covered, and cover tightly.

Refrigerate

Step 2 - Method 2 - Vinegar-salt brine with spices

1. Finishing brine as in method 1.
2. Spices that may be added.

Amounts for 10 lbs. (4½ kg) fish

Allspice 1 to 3 oz.	1/3 to 1 cup	80 to 250 ml
Bay leaves 1 to 2 oz.	100 to 200 leaves	
Mustard seed ½ to 2 oz.	1½ to 6 tbs.	27 to 108 ml
Pepper corns 1 to 3 oz.	3 to 9 tbs.	54 to 162 ml
Cloves ½ to 1 oz.	2¼ to 4½ tbs.	40 to 80 ml
White pepper ½ to 1 oz.	2½ to 5 tbs.	45 to 90 ml
Fennel seed ½ to 1 oz.	2¼ to 4½ tbs.	40 to 80 ml
Paprika ¼ to 1 oz.	1 to 2 tbs.	18 to 36 ml
Pickling spices 1 to 4 oz.	¼ to 1 cup	65 to 250 ml
Onion powder 1 to 4 oz.	4 tbs. to 1 cup	65 to 250 ml
Juniper berries 1 to 2 oz.	1/3 to 2/3 cup	85 to 170 ml
Cinnamon stick 1 to 2 oz.		28 to 56 g.
Nutmeg ½ to 2 oz.	2¼ to 9 tbs.	40 to 160 ml
Sugar 1 oz. to 1 lb.	2 tbs. to 2 cups.	30 to 500 ml

Prepare finishing brine as in method 1, including sugar if desired (see note *), and your choice of above spices. SPICES should be sterilized before adding to pack, because they are usually primitively handled during production and can be a source of food spoilage organisms. To sterilize the spices either *simmer* them in the finishing brine for 45 minutes to extract the flavor, then strain the spices out and discard them, or bring brine and spices to a *boil* for 1 minute, cool, then add brine *and* spices to the pack. In either case be sure to *cool* brine before using.

* (Note) SUGAR added to soften the bite of the vinegar can ferment and spoil the pack *if* the marinade is *not* kept refrigerated. Commercial marinade producers, whose products often are not refrigerated, lean toward using artificial sweeteners instead. If you decide to use a substitute for sugar, follow guidelines on the sweetener label, and experiment on a small pack first.

Pack the fish according to instruction for method 1.

Step 2 - Method 3 - Vinegar-salt brine with vegetable garnishes and spices

1. Pickling Brine as in Step 1 (for vegetables)
2. Finishing Brine with spices as in method 2.

Vegetables that may be used

celery - 1 x 1½ in. pieces	sweet peppers - rings
carrots - strips	onions - rings
mushrooms - small, whole, lg. cut	chilis - small whole, lg. cut

1. **Vegetables** to be used as garnishes must be blanched to remove oxygen that would encourage the growth of spoilage organisms. Steam celery, carrots, mushrooms, and sweet peppers until tender. Roast thick skinned peppers in a 400° F oven until skin chars, rub skin off and rinse. Thin skinned chilis and onions need no blanching.

2. **Pickle vegetables,** before adding to the pack so that they will not take

1.

2.

vinegar and salt from the Finishing Brine and dilute it with their water. Use the same pickling brine ratio as was used for the fish in step 1; e.g. 3½ oz. pickling salt disolved in 32 oz. of 5% vinegar. Pour brine over prepared vegetables and allow at least 3 days for the pickling to be complete at room temperature, or a week in the refrigerator. Stir vegetables occasionally during the pickling process.

3. **Prepare finishing brine** as in method 2.

4. **Drain vegetables** from their *pickling* brine.

5.   6.

5. **Choose glass containers** for this pack because you have the opportunity to create a *show piece*. Use your artistry in arranging the fish and vegetables to make an attractive pack.

6. **Cover the pack** with the spiced brine. Be sure you exclude any air trapped in the pack.

7. **Seal.**

8. **Refrigerate.**

Step 2 - Method 4 - Covering sauce

1. **Vegetables are often included** when packing fish with a covering sauce. If you choose to include them, prepare and pickle them as instructed in method 3.

2. **Covering sauce** can be chosen from those given in chapter 23.

3. **Pack the fish** (and vegetables) into any vinegar proof container, cover with the Covering Sauce and seal. As these sauces are all opaque; there isn't the opportunity to create a showpiece with this pack.

4. **Refrigerate.**

Chapter **21**

Cooked marinades

Cooked marinades keep better because the heat of cooking destroys many of the causes of spoilage. By the same token, the heat also destroys many of the enzymes that could *ripen* the fish and improve its flavor, so you have to depend more on spices to help with the flavoring.

Cooked marinades are made in two steps

Step 1. Poach fish in a vinegar salt cooking brine.
Step 2. Pack poached fish is vinegar-salt covering brine, or in a covering sauce.

Before proceeding with these directions please read through both steps to see what preliminary preparation (e.g. preparation of vegetables) are necessary.

Step 1.   Poaching fish

Prepare the fish.

Fillet large fish (see chapter 4). Cut fins off small fish and cut fish in serving size pieces.

Soak out any remaining blood because it will turn dark. Use a *cool* 35° salinometer deblooding brine and soak for 30 minutes.

35 ° sal. brine

Pickling salt	Water
2 oz. (¼ Cup)	20 oz.
or	
60 g. (60 ml)	600 ml

Drain the fish well after soaking.

Skin fillets and cut them into small serving pieces or into bite-size chunks in preparation for cooking.

Cooking the fish

The cooking brine is: 3 parts water
2 parts 5% vinegar
6% pickling salt

Cooking Brine

Pickling salt	5% vinegar	Water
6 oz. (¾ cup)	40 oz.	60 oz.
	or	
180 g (180 ml)	1200 ml	1800 ml

Cook the fish by simmering-*don't* boil it. The commercial processor keeps the cooking liquid at 185° F - (85°C). Simmer the fish until tender when tested with a fork - from 5 to 15 minutes according to thickness. I find it convenient to cook fish in about 2 lb. (1 kg) batches in 100 oz. of brine.

After cooking, remove the fish from the cooking brine, and rinse with a spray of water to remove any cooking scum and to cool the fish. At this time bone the chunks of small fish.

Re-use the cooking brine, because even salt is expensive now. Of course the fish will have taken vinegar and salt out of the brine; the next batch of fish wouldn't be properly processed if you used it without bringing it back to strength. So replenish the salt and vinegar.

Replenish for each 2 lb. batch of fish by adding

Pickling salt	5% Vinegar
2 tsp.	4 oz.
or	
10 g (10 ml)	120 ml

Step 2. Packing fish

You may choose one of these methods for packing
1. Vinegar-salt, spiced jell
2. Vinegar-salt brine
3. Covering sauce.
Pickled vegetables may also be included in any of the above.

The masterpiece of cooked marinades, and my favorite European cooked marinade, is one in which the fish and vegetable garnishes are molded in a spiced, jell brine. Since this is not only delicious but most attractive for special occasions, I will concentrate on its preparation. I won't neglect the other packing choices, though; they are merely off shoots of the *masterpiece.*

PACKING IN A VINEGAR-SALT JELL

Vegetable garnishes are important to marinades for taste and eye appeal. The vegetables must be *prepared* for packing with the fish, however; otherwise they would spoil the keeping qualities of the pack.

Vegetable preparation includes:

1. Cutting Vegetables to appropriate size for garnishing.
2. Blanching to remove oxygen.
*   3. Pickling

Appropriate vegetables and the above operations, *except* for pickling*, are covered in chapter 20. Please turn there for direction.

*The brine formula you must use for pickling these vegetables is the same as you use for packing this marinade, i.e. the *covering brine* that follows.

The Covering Brine formula is: 3 parts water
2 parts 5% vinegar
2½% pickling salt

Prepare covering brine using

Pickling salt	5% Vinegar	Water
2.6 oz. (1/3 cup)	40 oz.	60 oz.
	or	
75 g (75 ml)	1200 ml	1800 ml

Pickle the prepared vegetables, in enough of this brine to cover, for at least 3 days at room temperature, or up to a week in the refrigerator (I keep a jar of garnishing vegetables in the fish frig. ready to be used at anytime).

Preparing the packing jell

This Packing Jell is made using Covering Brine as a base, spices and sugar if desired, and gelatin.

Equal weights of packing jell and fish - vegetable combination are necessary for good keeping quality. Therefore, maintain this ratio:

Fish-vegetable combination	Jellied Brine
1 lb.	16 oz.
or	
500 gm	500 ml

To add spices, select from the list in chapter 20. (Otherwise, proceed to instructions for adding gelatin).

To destroy any bacteria on the spices, and to extract their essence, crush and *simmer* them in the required amount of Covering Brine for 45 minutes. If you wish to sweeten the brine, add sugar of other sweetner, to suit your taste.

Let the brine settle, then decant carefully through a cloth - covered strainer or funnel. For a really clear jell filter the brine through a coffee filter (very slow!) or a kitchen paper towel (faster).

Add the gelatin to the *cooled* brine. This jell is much stronger than that used for other purposes. Use these proportions of brine to gelatin:

Covering brine	Gelatin
25 oz	1 oz. (4 envelopes)
or	
750 ml	28 g (4 envelopes)

Sprinkle the gelatin over the brine in a saucepan. Place over low heat and stir constantly until no granules are visible. Remove from heat, cool, and go on to Packing Instructions which follow.

Packing the Marinade

Containers for the jellied marinade must be acid and salt resistant. A stainless steel bowl is the easiest to *unmold,* but when making the marinade I like to make a number of servings, then refrigerate them for future use. Not having, nor wishing to use for storage if I had, a number of stainless bowls, I use large (2 lb.) plastic margarine containers. These are tapered just right for easy unmolding.

Placing the fish and garnishes by hand is necessary if you want an attractive finished mold. This is time consuming, but that's what makes similar commercial marinades so expensive.

Cool the container and keep it cool, while packing, by placing it in a bowl of ice. If you are packing a number of molds, refrigerate all those except the one you are packing.

Keep the jell at a temperature where it will just pour, warming it *slightly* if necessary, during the packing.

1.   Coat the bottom of the container with packing jell - about ¼ inch (7 mm) deep, and cool to jell.

2.   Arrange pickled vegetables in an attractive pattern on the bottom jelly. When you unmold the marinade for serving, this decorative garnish will then be on top.

3.   Cover the vegetable layer with a layer of jell and cool to set.

4.   Next arrange fish pieces on the layer of jelly; cover them with jell, and let set.

5. Depending on the size of the container, you can continue to pack alternate layers of vegetables ...

6. ... and fish.

7. Just be sure that the pieces in the top layer are well covered with jelly, otherwise they will spoil.
    Refrigerate the marinade and enjoy in the months ahead.

PACKING IN AN UNJELLIED BRINE

Place fish, and pickled vegetables if you wish, in any acid and salt resistant container.

Cover with the plain covering brine or covering brine with added spices and/or sweetner. Be sure all fish and vegetables are completely covered with brine.

Refrigerate.

PACKING IN A COVERING SAUCE

Pack fish with or without vegetable garnishes in an acid resistant container. Cover completely with one of the Covering Sauces - see recipes given in chapter 23. Since the Covering Sauces are all opaque there is no need to create a showy pack.

Chapter **22**

Fried
marinades

Contents

Why are Fried marinades different than cooked ones? For the same reason that any *fried* food tastes differently than *boiled* or poached - the difference is the *browning* that comes from frying. Often Fried food is not recognizable as the same food when boiled, but each cooking method has its admirers.

Two kinds of Fried Marinades

I classify Fried marinades into:
a. Mediterranean
b. Northern European

Mediterranean Fried Marinades are know as *Escabeches*. They are characterized by being covered with a zesty Mediterranean - type sauce, and you usually eat them *within days* after their preparation.

Nothern European Fried Marinades are typically covered with a plain or spiced vinegar - salt brine, or by a variety of sauces. You usually make them for *longer term* keeping.

Two steps to make Fried Marinades:

Step 1.   Bread or dust fish then pan or deep fry.

Step 2.   Cover fried pieces with a covering sauce or brine.

Prepare fish

Both Mediterranean and Northern European fried marinades get the same preparation for step 1.

Fillet the fish. (see chapter 4). Take fins off small fish then cut into serving size pieces. Skin fillets and cut them into serving or eating size pieces.

MAKING ESCABECHE-MEDITERRANEAN FRIED MARINADE

Step 1. - Escabeche

To prepare for frying you can simply dry the fish pieces, or you can dip them in milk then dust with flour.

Pan fry the fish pieces until just light brown. As you might expect from the origin of this marinade, olive oil, alone or with vegetable oil is a favorite for frying. Remove the fried pieces from pan, then drain and cool them.

Step 2. - Escabeche

Many cookbooks have recipes for Escabeche - they are all different. I have decided, rather than give you my choice of ingredients, to give a variety and let you choose ones which appeal to you.

Acidity strength (vinegar - lemon juice - white wine) will govern the keeping life of the marinade. You can suit your taste, keeping in mind that the *more acid* will keep longer.

Ingredients for Escabeche Covering Sauce

(for 2 lbs. or 1 kg of fish)

Optional:

2 or 3 chilis	¼ tsp. marjoram
½ tsp. dry red peppers	¼ tsp. paprika
1 or 2 cloves garlic (minced)	¼ tsp. cumin seed
2 tbs. parsley	½ tsp. oregano
tabasco or cayenne to taste	1 or 2 bay leaves
½ tsp. freshly ground pepper	½ tsp. coriander seed
salt to taste	ripe olives

Basic: 1 medium onion or equivalent amount of scallions or green onions
½ to 1 cup wine vinegar - white wine and lemon juice may be substituted
1 tsp. vegetable oil

Start by sauteing the chopped onions in the oil until just tender (yellow).

Add the vinegar or white wine and lemon juice or a combination of all three. Then add your choice of the other ingredients.

Simmer the sauce for 30 minutes.

Arrange the fried fish pieces in a deep dish (ceramic or glass).

Cover the fish with the hot sauce.

Cool then refrigerate at least overnight before serving; several days would be better. The greatest amount of vinegar indicated, will give a refrigerator shelf life of about 3 weeks.

Serve Escabeche on a bed of lettuce garnished with any or all of the following:
ripe olives
green onions (long shreds)
lemon or lime quarters

NORTHERN EUROPEAN FRIED MARINADES

These are different from Escabeches in that they are usually breaded and are often covered by a brine; occasionally, though, you cover them with a sauce.

Prepare fish

The preparation of the fish before going on to step 1 is described before instruction for making Escabeche; Please see.

Step 1. - Northern fried marinades

Flour for breading can be any kind you like. Commercial marinaders, in Europe, commonly use 50% wheat and 50% rye flour.

Bread the fish after draining them well; the pieces should be just moist enough for the flour to stick.

For a good coating, rest the breaded pieces for an hour, remoisten them with water then rebread.

Pan or deep fry? You can get the best flavor from pan frying in vegetable oil, but deep fat frying may be more convenient for you.

Deep fat fry, if this is your choice, at 350° F. (180° C). You can tell when the fish is cooked, because it will have lost enough moisture, at this point, to float.

Drain and cool the fried fish.

Step 2. - Northern fried marinades

Covering brine or sauce?

If a covering *brine* is your choice, you can vary the acidity, that preserves the fish, to suit your palate. As explained before, you control keeping time by acidity; the stronger the acidity the longer the life. Covering *sauce* formulas are made acid enough to keep marinades for several months or more, under refrigeration. The other ingredients in the sauces effectively modify the acidity to suit the average taste.

Covering Brines

Ingredients of covering brines are:
a. Vinegar
b. Salt
c. Spices
d. Sugar or other sweetner

Acidity can be varied to suit your taste, as explained earlier, but *salt must then also be varied.* Salt preserves but makes the fish *tough* - vinegar preserves also, but makes the fish *soft.* To get preservation *and* a desirable texture in the fish, you must keep salt and vinegar in balance. To save you from trial and error and many unsatisfactory batches of marinade, the following tables have been worked - out.

Vinegar - salt balance table

Acidity	5% Vinegar	Pickling Salt	Water
2.0%	40 oz.	3 oz. - wt. or liq.	60 oz.
	or	or	or
	1200 ml	90 g (90 ml)	180 ml
2.5%	50 oz.	3½ oz. - wt. or liq.	50 oz.
	or	or	or
	1500 ml	105 g (105 ml)	1500 ml
3.0%	60 oz.	4 oz. - wt. or liq.	40 oz.
	or	or	or
	1800 ml	120 g (120 ml)	1200 ml
3.5%	70 oz.	4½ oz. - wt. or liq.	30 oz.
	or	or	or
	2100 ml	135 g (135 ml)	900 ml

Spices are usually added to the above brines. Pick yours from the list in chapter 19. Simmer them in the brine for 45 minutes, strain them out, and discard.

Sugar or other sweetner can be added to the brine before simmering.

Cool the brine.

Pack the fish pieces in acid and salt proof containers - glass, plastic, etc. don't overpack the containers; there should not be more than *2 parts fish* to *1 part brine* for preservation.

Pour the cooled brine over the fish and let stand for 2 or 3 hours. During this time the fish will absorb the brine to compensate for the moisture lost during frying. Be sure the fish is covered with brine; any pieces exposed to the air will spoil. Cover the containers to prevent brine evaporation.

Refrigerate the marinade to increase the keeping time.

COVERING SAUCES

If you prefer a sauce to the covering brines described above, see the formulas in chapter 23.

Chapter **23**

Sauces for the marinades

The sauce recipes given are designed to give the necessary acidity to keep marinades for several months under refrigeration.

You can see that there are varying amounts of vinegar in the different recipes. The amount needed to give the necessary acidity for good refregerator life depends on other ingredients in the recipe. Some ingredients add acidity (tomato puree and wine for example). Other ingredients reduce acidity (by buffering).

These recipes will serve as a guide for you to concoct your own. When in doubt as to acidity, add *more* vinegar; most of the sauce recipes given, are only slightly acid tasting because of the *softening* effect of the other ingredients.

Mustard Sauce

1 oz. (2 tbs.) sugar (36 ml)
1 oz. (4 tbs.) dry mustard (72 ml)
2 oz. (6 tbs.) flour (108 ml)

½ oz. (3 tsp.) salt (54 ml)
½ tsp. tumeric (3 ml)

Blend into:
    12 oz. water (360 ml)
Cook and stir until thick then blend in:
    12 oz. 5% vinegar (360 ml)
Cook and stir until thick then melt in:
    ½ tbs. margarine (9 ml)
Will pack 2 pints of fish.

Tomato Sauce

Combine dry ingredients:

1½ tsp. sugar (9 ml)
½ tsp. garlic powder (3 ml)

2 tsp. salt (12 ml)
½ tsp. pepper (3 ml)

Blend into:

4 oz. water (120 ml)

Cook and stir until thick and blend in:
    11 oz. tomato paste (330 ml)   10 oz. 5% vinegar (300 ml)
Cook until thick.
Will pack 2 pints of fish.

Wine Sauce

Combine dry ingredients:

2½ tbs. sugar (45 ml)
2½ tbs. flour (45 ml)
3 tbs. powdered milk (54 ml)

3 tsp. salt (18 ml)
pinch cinnamon
pinch cloves

Blend into:

6 oz. water (180 ml)   4 oz. vegetable oil (120 ml)

Heat until thick then blend in:

6 oz. dry white wine (180 ml)   6 oz. 5% vinegar (180 ml)
3 tbs. tomato puree (54 ml)

Cook until thick.
Will pack 2 pints of fish.

Pepper Sauce

Blend dry ingredients:

2½ tbs. sugar (45 ml)
1½ tbs. potato flour (27 ml)
1½ tbs. wheat flour (27 ml)
4½ tbs. powdered milk (81 ml)
3 tsp. salt (18 ml)

1 tbs. red pepper or cayenne (6 ml)
1½ tsp. worcestershire (9 ml)
¼ tsp. onion powder (1.5 ml)
¼ tsp. garlic powder (1.5 ml)

Blend into:

10 oz. water (300 ml)   1 tsp. vegetable oil (6 ml)

Heat until thickened then blend in:

7 oz. 5% vinegar (210 ml)   3 oz. tomato puree (90 ml)

Will pack 2 pints of fish.

Mixed Pickle Sauce

Blend dry ingredients:

3½ tsp. sugar (21 ml)   3 tsp. salt (18 ml)
2½ tsp. flour (15 ml)   ¼ tsp. curry powder (1.5 ml)
3 tbs. powdered milk (54 ml)

Blend into:

6 oz. water (180 ml)

Heat until thickened then blend in:

2 oz. white wine (60 ml)   6 oz. 5% vinegar (180 ml)

Cook until thick then stir in:

6 oz. chopped mixed pickles (180 ml)

Then melt in:

2 tsp. margarine (12 ml)

Will pack 2 pints of fish.

Sweet and Sour Sauce

Combine dry ingredients:

5 oz. sugar (150 ml)   3 tsp. salt (18 ml)
3 tbs. powdered milk (54 ml)   1 tbs. corn starch (18 ml)
1½ tbs. flour (27 ml)

Blend into:

2 oz. water (60 ml)   4 oz. apple juice
2 oz. tomato puree (60 ml)   concentrate (120 ml)

Cook until thick.

Add:

6 oz. 5% vinegar (180 ml)   5 tbs. chopped raisins (90 ml)
4½ tbs. chopped almonds (81 ml)

Cook until thick.

4
SALTING

CONTENTS

Chapter **24**

How to salt

"Salted fish are as outdated as buggy whips". That statement pretty well sums up the attitude of most people toward the oldest form of fish preserving. Don't dismiss the subject so readily, however; how about caviar made from salted salmon or trout roe. Red caviar, as it is called, is second only in popularity to the preciously prices sturgeon variety. And how about Gravlax? That immensly popular Scandinavian taste treat is salted (with sugar) salmon or trout. Last but not least is the top delicatessen treat of North America - Lox; salted salmon (or trout).

A little realized fact, today, is that there are many delicious and exciting cooked dishes that can be made from salted salmon and trout, and under certain circumstances salting of these fish is very useful. Salting is as modern as tomorrow for several reasons: There are times, especially today with increased fishing pressure, when fishing is great in remote areas, but how can you get the fish home unspoiled? *Salt it!* Secondly, the *curing* that goes on in salted fish can create entirely new flavors - very desirable flavors. So, let me tell you how you can put the ancient art of salting to modern use.

Salted fish and health

Before going any further into salting fish, I'd like to put your mind at ease about salt and health problems. Because of an inherited high blood pressure problem, I am very aware of the hazards of too much dietary salt. But that doesn't stop me from enjoying salted fish. You see, the salt merely preserves the fish until I am ready to use it. Then I wash out the salt - removing as little or as much as I wish - all of it, if necessary.

Better quality possible from salting than freezing

In addition to my contention that salting sometimes offers the only simple way to get fish home in good condition, I say salting can often be *better than freezing*. I know that last is a bold statement; let me tell why I make it. Most people think that sticking a fish in one of those big white boxes called a home freezer performs some sort of preserving magic. They are highly misguided. For instance I live in an area of fish camps. The camps usually maintain home freezers for their customers' convenience. The fishermen wrap fish, then plunk them into the bowels of the freezer. All day and half of the night, people are constantly putting and taking fish. On a good fishing day, tremendous loads of fish go into the freezer. What's wrong with that? Just this: Food technologists know that fish, to yield an acceptable thawed product, must be *quick frozen*. *Quick frozen* means the fish must be cooled down to 23° F (-3° C) in *4 hours*. The fish I've described in those freezers sometimes don't get frozen for a week! Then people wonder why they taste like a salted and peppered brown paper bag. If freezing conditions like these are all that are available, you will find that *salted* fish provide a better end product than badly frozen ones.

New flavors from salted fish

My second contention: that salted fish acquires exciting new *cured* flavors, is verified by the fact that salt fish are highly priced delicatessen items. If you are unsure about enjoying cured flavors, how about the cured flavors in cheeses, in hams, in bacon, and in corned beef? So why not in fish?

How salting both preserves and changes flavor

Bacteria that spoil fish have no mouths; they absorb food through their skins (cell walls). Salt prevents bacteria from absorbing food; consequently they can't multiply, so no spoilage! Flavor change comes from the action of enzymes changing the fish protein into other, different tasting products. Salting, unlike freezing or canning, does not kill or disable enzymes, hence, new flavors!

Salting

Salmon and trout are, for the most part, fatty fish. If exposed to the air, their fat (unsaturated) quickly goes rancid. To prevent rancidity in salted fish, salt them in a brine and keep them submerged - away from the air.

Containers for brine salting

Where salmon and trout are concerned, you will be brine salting. This means that if you are going on a trip that might involve you in salting some fish, go prepared. Have the necessary containers along, and, of course, some salt.

The containers must be salt proof, so this means glass, ceramic, plastic, stainless or enameled steel. Plastic containers are certainly a natural for traveling, but be sure that you choose ones with tight fitting lids. Such lids are necessary to keep brine from spilling and to help in keeping the fish submerged.

Salting pieces of fillets enables you to safely bring home fish in good condition. Small containers can handle a quantity of fish yet fit easily into a refrigerator or ice chest.

About salt

Salt quality is important. Impurities in salt can discolor fish, slow salt penetration, cause fish to be tough, and, most importantly, they can give fish a bitter flavor. Use only pure pickling salt. It's usually available everywhere.

Two kinds of brine salting

You have two options in brine salting: 1. *Hard* salting. 2. *Mild* salting.
Mild salting requires refrigeration; *hard* salting does not.
Mild salted fish have more cured flavor than *hard* salted because they are more able to *ferment.*
Mild salted fish freshen (desalt) easier than *hard* salted.

HOW TO MILD SALT

Clean, and ice the fish if you can't salt right away, then salt as soon as possible. See cleaning instuctions chapter 1, and icing instruction chapter 2.

Fillet the fish. See chapter 3 for illustration.

Cut whole large fillets because it is impractical for the sport fishermen to refrigerate a container large enough to hold whole sides in brine. I suggest that you cut the whole fillets into pieces according to thickness - see chapter 6.

Score the skin on thick pieces, expecially if the pieces are large, so the salt can penetrate; make the scores about 1 inch long, and about 1½ inches apart. Cut just through the skin into the fatty layer below. See chapter 8.

A *Cold deblooding bath* is used by Commercial salters to *caseharden* the fish. Put the pieces in a *cold* 65° salinometer brine for 1 hour to keep fat fish from oozing oil. Also press out any remaining blood in this bath.

65 ° salinometer bath

Pickling Salt	Water
21 oz. (2 2/3 cups)	100 oz.
600 g (600 ml)	3 l

Drain the pieces well coming out of the bath.

Weigh the fish now so that you know how much salt to use for curing. Remember this is a *mild* cure and the salt must be limited so the fish will *cure*. Use the proportion of 1 lb. of pure *pickling salt* for each *10 lbs.* of *fish.*

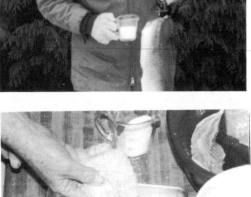

To salt the fish spread the required amount of salt in a pan or tray. Lay each piece of fish, skin side down on the salt and scoop the salt over it; *don't rub it in,* just cover the piece.

Pick up the piece with as much salt as will adhere to it and place it skin side down in the curing container.

When a layer of pieces is finished, sprinkle it lightly with salt. Remember the *total* salt, including that adhering to the fish and that sprinkled on the layers, is 1 lb. for each 10 lbs. of fish.

Pack the fish in successive layers, skin side down, until the top layer - pack it skin side up.

Fill the packed container with saturated brine - 100° sal.

Saturated brine

Pickling Salt	Water
36 oz. (4½ cups)	100 oz.
1020 g (1020 ml)	3 l

Weight or otherwise submerge the fish completely in the brine. Cover the container to keep out dirt and insects, and to stop brine from evaporating.

Store the container at 35 to 40° F. (2 to 4° C) - normal refrigerator temperature.

You can freshen and use the fish at any time, but it won't be cured and have full flavor until it has been in the brine for at least 2 weeks.

Use the fish within a year; after a year it will be hard to freshen.

Use mild salted fish for smoking as Old Fashioned Lox, see chpter 11. It can also be used very effectively in any of the recipes given in chapters 24 & 25.

HOW TO HARD SALT

Follow the same instructions as for *mild* salting, except use *2½ lbs.* of salt per 10 lbs. of fish.

It is not necessary to dredge the pieces in the salt; just sprinkle the salt on the bottom of the container and on the layers of fish.

Let the container stand overnight, if the fish doesn't make enough brine to cover, fill with the same saturated brine as used for the mild cure.

The container can be slightly overfilled when packing. As the fish stands overnight, it will settle and then fit the container.

Submerge fish completely in brine and cover.

Keep in a cool place, expecially during hot weather.

Fish are best if used within 1 year.

Chapter **25**

Japanese recipes for salted fish

Because salting was the major method of preservation in the early days, many nations used salted fish in their cookery. But few had the number of recipes for using salted trout and salmon that the Japanese enjoyed.

At one time Japan had abundant supplies of Pacific Salmon and sea-going trout in her own waters but when heavy use of the fish reduced home stocks, the Japanese imported large quantities of salt-preserved salmon from North America. In fact, most such products were exported, and few North Americans became familiar with them.

Because of this unfamiliarity, I am giving more recipes for using salted salmon and trout than for using more familiar products like smoked or pickled fish. I hope you will try and enjoy the exotic Japanese recipes as well as those from other parts of the world.

Please note that the recipes all require freshening the fish before use.

Freshen the fish in cold running water or in frequent changes of water until salt is removed to suit your taste. (Don't be repulsed by the thought of tasting raw fish; simply taste it; you needn't swallow it!). Remember that larger pieces of fish can take as long as 24 hours to desalt. It's better that a finished dish need salting than be overly salty, so don't stop the freshening process too soon.

JAPANESE INGREDIENTS

Daikon - Japanese white radish
Goma - Sesame seed
Koji - Lees from fermenting saki
Konbu - Kelp seaweed
Mirin - Sweet sake (medium dry sherry could be used)
Miso - Soy bean paste
Nori - Laver seaweed
Ocha - Green tea

Rice Vinegar - White vinegar may substitute, but is 10% stronger than rice vinegar
Sake - Rice wine
Sake malt
Shiromiso - White bean paste
Sasa - Bamboo leaves
Shoyu - Soy sauce
Usu Kuchi - Light soy sauce
Wasabi - Powdered horseradish

Basic preparations for Japanese recipes

Dashi

Soup stock made from katsuobushi (shaved, dried, smoked, bonito) or hanakatsuo (shaved dried fish).

To prepare Dashi

6 cups boiling water (1440 ml)
½ cup shaved katsuobushi or hanakatsuo (120 ml)

5 sq. in. konbu (kelp seaweed) (62 sq. cm.)

Stir kelp in boiled water for several minutes, remove, add shaved fish, bring to boil again, remove from heat, steep 2 minutes, strain, use broth.
Dashi Substitute - chicken broth with green onions and fresh ginger root added.

Sushi Rice

1½ cups rice (360 ml)
1¾ cups water (420 ml)
1 tbs. sugar (15 ml)

1/6 cup rice vinegar (40 ml)
optional: kombu (kelp) 2 in. piece

Wash rice and drain 1 hour. Bring to boil rice, water and kelp, remove kelp, cover pan, simmer rice 'til barely tender (15 min.), remove from heat and stand for 10 min. Meanwhile bring vinegar, salt and sugar to boil in another pan and remove from heat.

Place rice in bowl, sprinkle vinegar mix over, and mix into rice. Best sushi rice is quickly cooled by fanned cold air while cutting in vinegar mix - a glossy sheen is desirable.

Ishikari - Nabe

8 oz. freshened salmon
  or trout (225 g)
⅓ cup Japanese radish (80 ml)
⅔ cup carrots (160 ml)
⅓ cup leeks (80 ml)

⅔ cup potato (160 ml)
2 tsp. mirin (sweet saki) (10 ml)
2 tbs. soy sauce (30 ml)
6 cups dashi (soup stock) (1440 ml)
2 tsp. sake (rice wine) (10 ml)

Bring Dashi or chicken stock to boil, add vegetables cut in ½ inch pieces, simmer until close to tender, add seasonings and fish. Cook fish only 10 minutes per inch of thickness.

Mimaki - Zushi

½ lb. sliced freshened salmon
  or trout (225 g)
½ cup vinegar (120 ml)

2 tbs. sugar (30 ml)
8 cups sushi rice (2 l)
8 sheets nori (laver)

Marinate slices of fish in vinegar, sugar, (salt to taste), for 30 minutes, drain.

Toast Nori leaves by passing over stove burner until crisp, cover all but top portion with 1 cup sushi rice.

Divide marinated salmon between the 8 spreads.

Place Nori leaves on bamboo table mat or similar, and roll, lightly packing ingredients. Unspread part of leaf will cover.

Slice rolls into 1 inch pieces with dampened knife - Serve.

Kogane - Yaki

6 freshened salmon or trout
  serving portions
1 egg yolk

salt to taste
chopped parsley
1 tsp. mirin (5 ml)

Mix egg yolk, mirin, salt.

Preheat broiler, brush fish portions with egg mix, broil 10 minutes per inch of thickness, turning at half time. Brush with egg mix on both sides 'til mix used.

Serve garnished with chopped parsley. For a special touch uni (sea urchin) may be mixed with the egg to form the glaze.

A variation of egg-glazed broiled fish is:

Teriyaki Broiled

Teriyaki sauce (ready made) or to make mix:
6 tbs. dark soy sauce (90 ml)	6 tbs. saki (90 ml)
6 tbs. mirin (90 ml)	1 clove garlic (chopped finely)

Sakana Misozuke (cured, broiled)

1 lb. freshened salmon or trout serving pieces (450 g)	⅓ cup mirin (80 ml)
	2 tbs. sake (30 ml)
1 lb. shiromiso (white bean paste) (450 g)	

Mix bean paste, mirin, and sake and spread half on bottom of a baking dish.

Place fish on paste and cover with remaining paste mix. Cure in refrigerator from overnight to several days.

Wipe paste mix from fish and bake or broil for 10 minutes per inch of thickness.

For a special touch, sandwich the fish in sasa (bamboo leaves) for baking.

This may be served at once but is also excellent cold in salad such as daikon (Japanese radish) salad seasoned with salt, sugar, vinegar and red pepper.

Ocha - Chazuke (soup)

sliced, freshened, broiled salmon or trout	2 cups ocha (green tea) (480 ml) or
3 cups cooked (hot) rice (720 ml)	2 cups dashi or
2 sheets nori (laver)	2 cups chicken broth
1 tsp. salt	2 tbs. powdered horseradish (30 ml)
	1 tbs. light shoyu (soy sauce) (15 ml)

Cook rice, broil fish lightly. Toast nori over burner.

Make horseradish paste with water and add to ocha in saucepan; add salt, shoyu; simmer 10 minutes.

Place rice in bowl, place salmon slices on it, cover with the liquid, and crumble the toasted nori over all.

Unchu - Yaki (baked)

3 cups plain boiled rice (720 ml)	1 cup dashi or chicken broth (240 ml)
½ lb. freshened salmon or trout slices (225 g)	1 tbs. mirin (15 ml)
1 egg white	1 tsp. salt (5 ml)
corn starch	

Press cooked rice with wet hands, into flat cakes, top with fish slices, brush with beaten egg white, broil or bake.

Add seasonings to dashi or broth and thicken with corn starch. Serve over baked fish.

Sanpei - Jiru (Stew)

½ lb. freshened salmon or trout
    pieces (225 g)
½ cup saki (120 ml)
¾ cup water (180 ml)
4 tbs. miso (60 ml)
1 tbs. sugar (15 ml)
1 tbs. shoyu (15 ml)

daikon
potatoes
carrots
celery
burdock root, etc.
fresh ginger root

Cut vegetables into ½ in. pieces and simmer in water, sake and sugar until nearly cooked, add fish and cook 10 minutes per inch of thickness.

Remove fish and keep warm. Add bean paste to liquid, heat and stir until dissolved, add shoyu and remove from heat.

Pour the sauce over fish in individual bowls and sprinkle grated ginger root over.

Sa - Tsu-Ma A-Ge

(deep-fried fish cake with chopped vegetables)

To make about two dozen:

1.5 kg (3½ lb.) cod or *salmon fillet
    bones should be removed. Cut
    into small pieces
4 tbs. cornstarch
2 tsp. sugar
1 tsp. MSG

⅔ cup water
¼ pc carrot
2 pc green onion
1 tsp. GO-MA (sesame seeds)
1 - 2 tsp. salt
1 egg

Mix cornstarch with some water to prevent lumping. Take the first 6 ingredients and mix in an electric mixer, or blender at low-medium speed for about 7 minutes.

Chop carrot and green onion together with sesame seeds. Mix into the main preparation.

Add salt little by little to harden the mixture.

Shape with hands into two dozen pieces and deepfry at medium heat in good cooking oil.

Serve hot or cold.

Recipe courtesy Minori Miki, Nanaimo, B.C.

*note-Freshened salted salmon may be used.

Chapter **26**

Recipes
of the world
for salted fish

Laksloda (Finland)

1 lb. salted salmon or trout (450 g) (freshened and sliced)	1 tbs. flour (15 ml)
	3 tbs. melted butter (45 ml)
4 medium potatoes (sliced)	2 tbs. butter (30 ml)
1 medium onion (sliced)	whole allspice
2½ cups light cream (600 ml)	salt and pepper
parsley	

Place potatoes, sliced fish, and onions in layers in a buttered casserole. Season each layer with salt and freshly ground pepper and sprinkle each layer with flour. End with a layer of potatoes and sprinkle it lightly with whole allspice.

Mix the cream and melted butter and pour it over the casserole, adding water if necessary to cover.

Dot with butter and bake at 325° F until potatoes are tender (about 1 hr).

Serve sprinkled with parsley.

Serves 6.

Fritters with Skorthalia (Greece)

1 lb. salted salmon or trout (450 g)
(freshened)

oil for deep frying
(preferably olive)

Skorthalia (Garlic Sauce)

4 large cloves garlic
(mashed and minced)
1 cup olive oil (240 ml)
2 egg yolks

2 tbs. white wine vinegar (30 ml)
1 tbs. lemon juice (15 ml)
1 tsp. salt (5 ml)
½ cup almonds (blanched,
lightly toasted, ground) (120 ml)

Batter

¼ cup flour (60 ml)
1¼ tbs. olive oil (20 ml)
salt

1 egg white
⅔ cup water (tepid) (160 ml)

Blanch almonds and toast in a 350° F oven until light brown. Grind almonds finely in a blender.

Make the garlic sauce by placing egg yolks, vinegar, lemon juice, garlic and salt in the blender. Blend, then at low speed gradually and steadily add oil. Add the almonds and stir into the sauce to thicken.

Next make the fritter batter by adding salt to the flour, add the oil and mix well, then add the water and beat thoroughly. Beat the egg white until stiff then carefully fold it into the batter.

Cut the fish into 2 in. pieces, dip in the batter, and fry a few pieces at a time in plenty of olive oil. Drain and keep warm.

Egg plant slices dipped in batter goes well with this dish, but will require doubling the batter recipe

Serve fish and eggplant with the Skorthalia.

Serves 4 to 6.

Lomi Salmon (Hawaii)

1 lb. salted salmon or trout (450 g)
(freshened)
5 large ripe tomatoes

1 medium onion (chopped finely)
1 bunch green onions (sliced
thinly long way)

Shred raw freshened fish.
Combine fish with rest of the ingredients and chill.
Serve with lettuce.
Serves 4.

Rougaille (Mauritius)

½ lb. salted salmon or trout
(450 g) (freshened)
¼ cup cooking oil (60 ml)
4 onions (chopped)
1 tsp. chopped parsely (5 ml)
4 scallions chopped

1 cup tomatoes (240 ml)
(chopped, or tomato juice)
1 clove garlic
½ tsp. ginger (3 ml)
1 hot pepper seeded and diced

Fry fish pieces lightly in oil, then add onions, parsley, scallions, tomatoes, and pepper. Cook until the onions are soft.

Add garlic and ginger and simmer about 5 to 10 minutes.

Serve with rice.

Serves 2.

Martinique Fishballs

2 lbs. salted salmon or trout	½ cup hot water (120 ml)
(freshened) (900 g)	¼ cup sifted flour (60 ml)
1 onion	pinch baking soda
pepper (freshly ground)	vegetable oil for deep fat frying
½ tsp. saffron (2.5 ml)	

Slice the onion into the poaching pan in enough water to cover the fish and cook for 10 minutes; add the fish and simmer until cooked.

Mash or chop the fish finely and season with pepper (and salt if necessary) to taste.

Dissolve the saffron in the water, then blend in the flour and baking soda to form a smooth paste.

Mix the paste with the fish, and shape into walnut size balls.

Fry a few balls at a time until golden brown.

Serve with a pepper sauce, e.g. chili sauce with red peppers.

Serves 6.

Jamaica Fritters

1 lb. salted salmon or trout (450 g)	3 eggs (beaten)
(freshened)	½ cup flour (120 ml)
1 clove garlic (minced)	3 tbs. butter (45 ml)
1 onion (finely chopped)	1 tomato (chopped)

Poach fish until cooked, then mash it finely.

Mix the mashed fish with the garlic, onion, tomato, and eggs.

Shape mixture into fritters, roll in flour, and fry in butter until golden brown all over.

Serve with boiled green bananas, or fried ripe ones.

Pouf (Italy)

1 lb. salted salmon or trout (450 g)	2 tsp. parsley (finely chopped)
(freshened)	(10 ml)
½ cup olive oil (120 ml)	2 tsp. lemon juice (10 ml)
½ cup milk (120 ml)	pepper (freshly ground)
2 cloves garlic (finely chopped)	½ cup white wine with enough
	water to cover fish (120 ml)

Place fish in poaching pan and cover with the *cold* wine and water mix. *Slowly* bring up to a boil, then drain fish.

Blend or grind fish to a very fine paste adding a little of the olive oil and milk at a time. When the mixture is smooth blend in the garlic, parsley, lemon juice and pepper and beat until fluffy.

Shape into a mound, refrigerate and serve with Italian bread, antipasto.

Al Acciuga (Italy)

1½ lb. salted salmon or trout   1½ tbs. flour (23 ml)
(675 ml) (freshened)   4 anchovy fillets
2 medium onions (chopped)   1 cup milk (240 ml)
½ cup olive oil (120 ml)   pepper (freshly ground)
1 tbs. parsley (minced) (5 ml)

Cook the onions in the olive oil until soft, add the chopped parsley, then blend in the flour.

Cut the fish into serving pieces and place in a baking dish. Cover the fish with the onion mix and cover this with the broken up anchovy fillets. Grind on pepper to taste then pour on milk.

Mix all together gently and bake at 275°F until the milk is absorbed (about 1 hr.).

Serves 4.

Com Pimentos e Tomatoes (Portugal)

1½ lb. salted salmon or trout   5 tomatoes (sliced)
(675 g) (freshened)   1 tsp. saffron (2 ml)
1 lb. potatoes (450 g)   black olives
5 tbs. olive oil (75 ml)   salt and pepper
4 green peppers (seeded and sliced)   1 cup white wine (240 ml)

Poach the fish in the white wine, plus enough water to cover, until *just* tender.

Cook potatoes (skin on) until *just* cooked.

Heat one tbs. olive oil in a casserole, and cook the peppers until limp then set them aside.

Place layers of peeled, sliced potatoes, fish, tomatoes, and peppers, season with salt, pepper, and saffron, and sprinkle with the balance of the olive oil. Bake in a 350°F oven until heated through and slightly browned.

Serve in the casserole, garnished with the black olives.

Serves 4.

Curried Salad

1 lb. salted salmon or trout (450 g)   ½ cup seedless raisins (120 ml)
(freshened)   ½ cup green onion (120 ml)
1 tbs. lemon juice (15 ml)   (chopped)
1 apple (diced)   1½ tsp. curry powder (8 ml)
1 cup celery top, stalk, and leaves,   1 tsp. garam masala (5 ml)
diced (240 ml)   ½ cup mayonnaise (120 ml)

Poach the fish until tender, drain then chill.

Dice the apple and sprinkle with lemon juice. Combine the apple, celery, raisins and green onion.

Mix the curry powder, or garam marsala (see an East Indian cookbook if you're curious) with the mayonnaise.

Combine the flaked fish with the other ingredients, and serve on lettuce.

Raito (Provence)

2 lbs. salted salmon or trout
(freshened) (900 g)
2 tbs. olive oil (30 ml)
2 large onions (chopped)
2 cloves garlic (chopped)
2 green peppers (chopped)
¾ cup black olives (chopped)
(180 ml)
5 bunches parsley (chopped)
3 tbs. capers (drained and
chopped) (45 ml)

¾ cup walnuts (pounded or
blended fine) (180 ml)
2 cups paste tomatoes (canned or
chopped fresh) (480 ml)
¾ cup dry red wine (180 ml)
2 bay leaves
1 tsp. thyme (5 ml)
1 tsp. rosemary (5 ml)
1 tsp. fennel (5 ml)

Cook the onions, garlic, and peppers in olive oil until tender. Add olives, tomatoes, wine (be sure not to cook wine sauce in iron or aluminum or else it will turn grey) bay leaves, thyme, rosemary, fennel, and capers and simmer for 2 hours.

Add fish cut into serving pieces and continue simmering until fish is cooked (flakes). Add walnuts to thicken the sauce, then serve garnished with chopped parsley. Adjust salt if necessary.

Serves 6.

Zapekanka (Russian)

½ lb. salted salmon or trout
(225 g) (freshened)
2 cups mashed potatoes (480 ml)
1 cup bread, soaked in milk,
squeezed out and torn (240 ml)
2 eggs separated
pepper

1 onion (chopped fine)
1 tbs. butter (15 ml)
¼ cup bread crumbs (60 ml)
½ cup sour cream (120 ml)
1 egg
¼ cup chopped parsley (60 ml)

Grind the fish or chop it finely, and mix it with the mashed potatoes, onion, bread and egg yolks, and season with pepper.

Beat the egg whites stiff and fold into the fish mix.

Butter a baking dish and sprinkle the butter with bread crumbs.

Spread mix in the dish about 2 in. (10 cm) deep.

Beat the remaining egg into the sour cream and spread over the casserole.

Bake in a 350° F oven until golden brown (20 to 30 minutes).

Cut into squares and serve with chopped parsley.

Serves 4.

Other salted Salmon or Trout Dishes

Newberg
Cakes (with mashed potatoes)
Scrambled in eggs

Vegetable pie
Stuffed baked potato
Brandaide

See recipes in the smoked salmon and trout section.

Chapter **27**

Caviar and
other salted roes

"Caviar" perhaps the one expression, if any, that can convey the thought of more gastronomic opulence than "Smoked Salmon". I doubt if caviar can be said to be more universally *liked* than smoked salmon, but for those who really appreciate caviar, and those who are impressed by its price, it stands alone at the top of the epicurean ladder. So much for the gourmet's near reverence for caviar - here is the point of interest for trout and salmon fishermen, and for special friends of the fishmonger: true caviar (sturgeon eggs) is a most imitated delicacy - and caviar made from salmon and trout is considered to be the *best* of the imitations.

By law, in th U.S., the *substitutes* for the roe of the sturgeon *may not* be labeled caviar. This is a labelling technicality, however, and for the sake of our discussion I will continue to describe the substitutes as caviar.

There is lump fish caviar, which makes up the bulk of the substitutes, then paddlefish caviar, and pollack, cod, vendace, and caviar made from just about any roe except the roe of the Pacific Cabezon which is reported to be poisonous. Of all these, the outstanding substitute is caviar from salmon and trout - Red Caviar.

Red Caviar devotees who pay over $15 for a tiny 4 ounce jar of this delicacy, would be horrified to see fishermen at the fishcamp, near me, feeding hundreds of pounds of salmon roe to the gulls every week. Especially so, if they knew the easy way of making red caviar, that I am about to describe. Following the instructions for Regular and Japanese Red Caviar, I'll tell of some ways of using Red Caviar, and then give directions for other products made from trout and salmon roe.

Fishermen feed hundreds of pounds of salmon roe to the seagulls.

Expensive gull fare

To make Red Caviar you will need a piece of ½ in. or ¼ in. mesh screen *at least* one foot square. (The size of the eggs will dictate the mesh size). Galvanized screen may be all that is available, but if you have a choice, plastic, plain steel, or stainless steel is preferable. Plain steel can be protected from rust with edible (cooking) oil or a coating of resin. If you must use galvanized screen coat it with resin too, to keep the eggs from direct contact with the galvanized coating.

1. Separating the eggs from the membrane that contains them is the first step; gently but firmly rub the skein of eggs over the screen.

2. Discard the membrane, blood vessels, etc. remaining on the screen after most of the eggs have passed through.

3. Make a 80° sal brine.

Pickling Salt	Water
8.6 oz. (1 cup, 2 tbs.)	1 qt.
or	
270 g (270 ml)	1 l

4. Gently stir the eggs in the *cooled* 80° brine from 15 to 30 minutes. The uptake of salt will depend on the maturity of the eggs. You can see when the eggs are salted enough because they begin to look opalescent. Remember the highest quality caviar is the lowest in salt. Too much salt will cover-up the delicate flavor of the eggs.

5. Drain the eggs after the brining; this takes at least 8 hours if there is any quanity of eggs. The caviar must be kept cool to prevent spoilage during draining, but *not too* cool. Temperature below 40° F (5° C) will cause the eggs to congeal and prevent good drainage. A refrigerator is *too* cool for this.

6. Pack the finished caviar in jars after draining. I find half pint mason jars to be a good size for the hors d'oeuvre for a large group. Smaller containers, such as baby food jars, etc. are good for smaller groups.

7. Refrigeration is extremely important for keeping caviar; the *ideal* temperature is 34° to 36° F (2 to 3° C). Below 29° F the caviar will freeze and turn into a worthless mass (don't throw it out, though, it is useful as a dip or flavoring); above 40° F it will have a very short shelf life. If the roes that you used for the caviar were fairly mature, there will be some fat and juice exude from them while the caviar is stored in the jar. Turn the jar over, from time to time, so that all the eggs get *bathed* in this juice. **Caution! Caviar kept in a sealed container must be refrigerated all the time! See chapter 33 for information on Botulism.**

8. Sterilization or pasteurization of Caviar may be recommended in other literature you read. Neither can be recommended for Red Caviar, however, based on experiments I have made. Pictured is one of the experiments run to find the effect of various heat treatments on shelf life and quality of red caviar.

9. Color of Red Caviar is progressively destroyed by heat treatment necessary to pasteurize or sterilize the pack. On the *right* is a jar of untreated red caviar. Notice how several heat treatments have partially, then almost completely destroyed the natural color in those jars to the left. *Rely on good refrigeration* practices instead!

JAPANESE RED CAVIAR

This caviar differs from Regular Red Caviar because it is *not* separated into individual eggs; the entire skein of roe is salted.

1. Shown here is a batch of roes from chum salmon. These were from commercially caught fish, late in the season, so the roes were really overly mature and loose for this style of red caviar.

2. To make Japanese red Caviar, first make a 100° Salinometer brine:

Pickling Salt	Water
36 oz.(4½ cups)	100 oz.
or	
1020 g (1020 ml)	3 l

The Japanese use 100 PPM nitrates to retain color, but I do not find this necessary.

3. Stir the skeins of eggs in the *cooled* 100° sal. brine for 30 minutes, then drain, in a cool place until the brine has stopped dripping.

4. This small packing box that I made for home use, is a substitute for the 10 kilo boxes used commercially for packing Japanese red caviar. I line the container with polyethylene sheeting or plastic wrap and place the brined skeins, distributing an additional 6 tsp. salt per pound of eggs over the skeins.

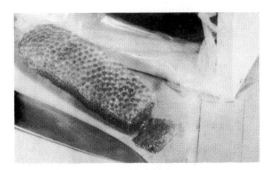

5. Commercial caviar producers over-pack the box, place the lid, then invert the box so the weight compresses the eggs to give form to the skeins. I fashioned a lid that fits inside my home box and used a 7 lb. downrigger weight to press and form the caviar

6. Cure the Caviar 1 to 2 weeks depending on the maturity of the eggs. Do this curing at ordinary refrigeration temperature. After curing you can slice the caviar for the uses suggested in chapter 28

Japanese red Caviar will keep for several months under refrigeration. For longer keeping, freeze it. Unlike the lighter-salted, regular red caviar, the Japanese product is not harmed by freezing.

BOTARGO

Botargo, boutargue, poutargue, bottarga, putago, or avgotaracho are different nations' names for a great Mediterranean delicacy; salted, dried, sausage-shaped roes of the grey mullet.

I have never tasted the real thing but I can't imagine it's being any better than the botargo made from salmon or trout roe. Like a dry salami, it can be sliced thin and eaten on bread and butter, or on toast, that's been dipped or fried in olive oil. A good dressing for it is either lemon juice, a vinaigrette, or a drop to two of olive oil.

Its piquancy reminds me of anchovy, and botargo can, like anchovies, work wonders in flavoring salads, vegetables, meat dishes, or pizza.

One of the best uses for botargo is in Taramasalata; see chapter 28.

Botargo slices like salami

Taramasalata from botargo

In the Mediterranean the roes are sun dried, but I find it easy to place the liberally salted roes on kitchen paper towels with an under layer of newspaper. As the salt extracts moisture from the roes and wets the towels, I replace them with fresh ones, until no further moisture comes out.

The first day after salting and starting to dry, the roes will have *slumped* - flattened out. Before they get any drier, roll them, while they are still pliable, into a sausage shape. Resalt if necessary and continue drying.

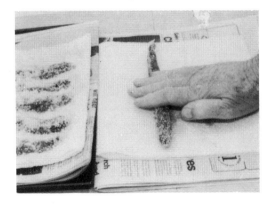

After the botargo is thoroughly dried they can be wrapped in film and stored in the fridge, or sealed by dipping in paraffin.

Chapter **28**

Serving caviar and other salted roes

SERVING REGULAR RED CAVIAR

There are rules for serving caviar that assure its enjoyment, and the serving of Red Caviar is no exception.

The first rule, if serving caviar as a canapé is to let your guests serve themselves, for there is nothing worse than a soggy bit of caviar - covered bread or toast.

Secondly, present the caviar in a glass or ceramic bowl, (never metal) surrounded by chopped ice. Even a sterling bowl in all its elegance is rejected by experts and they extend the ban to the serving spoon. A glass or bone spoon, is considered necessary, an ivory spoon, the ultimate. Masters of the hors d'oeuvre believe that caviar should be undressed - au naturel - served perhaps, with lemon quarters if the caviar is a bit salty. However, it is customary to surround the caviar with bowls of finely chopped onion, sour cream, chopped egg (the whites and yolks often served separately), chopped parsley or for the finest touch, a bowl of chopped breast of pheasant.

Serve with buttered rye bread or buttered *warm* toast (quartered or shaped) or best of all **Blini,**those little, light, Russian buckwheat pancakes that were invented, in the days of Czars to be heaped - up with caviar. Now let your quests enjoy their favourite combination or experiment with your offerings.

Other Red Caviar dishes for the hors d'oeuvre

If you want to prepare caviar for service ahead of time, there are interesting ways to bypass the canapé. These also may be more attractive to guests who "can't look those fish eggs in the eye".

Caviar Stuffed Eggs

1 tbs. caviar per egg 15 ml	chopped chives or green onion
½ tsp. each per egg	chopped parsley
mayonaise or sour cream	to taste - freshly ground pepper

Halve boiled eggs, scoop out yolks and mash with other ingredients, heap the filling back into the whites.

Serve decorated with mayonnaise or better still, Russian (caviar) dressing.

Russian Dressing

This is a dressing made with caviar. I have seen recipes that do awful things to destroy the caviar flavor in Russian Dressing: for example, adding barbecue sauce and ketchup.

For the best Russian Dressing make fresh mayonnaise and blend or mix in 2 tablespoons caviar per cup of mayonnaise. If you wish, add a teaspoon of horseradish and/or a teaspoon of grated onion.

Red Caviar on Smoked Salmon

Place a slice of salmon on rye bread, toast, or blin, then top with red caviar. Decorate with sour cream and embellish with chopped onion, parsley, egg, etc.

Red Caviar Stuffed Coronets

Mold slices of ham or Scotch smoked salmon inside a cornucopia mold to form a shell. Fill the shell with a mixture of mashed hard cooked egg and red caviar bound in mayonnaise.

Red Caviar with Oysters

Shuck the oysters and return the oyster to the *deep* part of its cleaned shell. Rim the shell with caviar and place a thin wedge of lemon on the oyster. Serve with bowls of chopped parsley and grated onion.

Caviar Dip

¾ cup red caviar 180 ml	1 cup sour cream 240 ml
chopped hard cooked egg	½ tsp. freshly ground
2 tbs. chopped onion 30 ml	black pepper 3 ml
2 oz. milk 60 ml	½ tsp. lemon juice 3 ml

Dilute the sour cream with milk, add other ingredients except chopped egg, mix and serve in bowl sprinkled with chopped egg.

Caviar - Cheese Mix

1 cup cream cheese 240 ml	1 tbs. chopped onion 15 ml
½ cup red caviar 120 ml	1 tsp. freshly ground
lemon juice	black pepper 5 ml

Cream cheese, add the red caviar, onion, pepper, and season with lemon juice. Serve with toast or crackers.

Caviar Omelet

Prepare omelet and spinkle red caviar on the eggs, fold, finish cooking, and serve with sour cream.

Caviar Stuffed Trout

The boned trout (method 2, chapter 5) are excellent for this preparation.

6 trout (about 10 in. or 25 cm)	1½ qt. salted water 1500 ml
2 cups white wine (dry) 480 ml	2 sliced carrots
2 sliced onions	6 oz. red caviar 180 ml
1 small bay leaf	

Combine the water and wine, add onions, carrots and bay leaf, bring to a boil, lower trout, cradled in cheese cloth into liquid, and *immediately* lower temperature to a simmer. Simmer fish 10 minutes per inch (25 mm) of thickness. Lift fish from the liquid, cool, then chill them. Skin fish leaving head and tail on, then stuff each with 2 tbs. caviar (30 ml). Decorate with parsley or celery slice *scales,* and serve with cucumber and tomato slices.

Molded Caviar Salad

8 hard cooked eggs	1 tbs. grated onion 15 ml

2 oz. red caviar 60 ml	1 tsp. dry mustard 2 ml
3 tbs. softened butter 45 ml	2 tbs. lemon juice 30 ml

Mash eggs and mix other ingredients with them. Oil a tall tapered drinking glass and *pack* the mix into it. Chill until *solid,* unmold, slice the roll, and serve the slices alternated with tomato slices.

Caviar Butter

2 oz. red caviar 60 ml	4 oz. butter 120 ml
1 tbs. lemon juice 15 ml	

Cream the butter and mix in other ingredients. Chill and form into balls, or other shapes, or spread on waxed paper, and roll into *sausage* shape, slice and use to garnish fish.

How to Make Blini

This small pancake or blin (pl. blini) can be used with caviar or other ingredients of the hors d'oeuvre. Most of the recipes allow for 3 *risings* of the dough; this is time consuming even though the recipes are not difficult. The following recipe is one used to hasten the process in professional kitchens. If you prefer the longer process, you will find examples in a number of good cookbooks.

1½ cups buchwheat flour or whole wheat 360 ml	4 eggs (separated)
1½ cups white flour 360 ml	1 tbs. active dry yeast 15 ml
	3 cups scalded warm milk 720 ml (110°F -45°C)

Place 1 cup of the warm milk in a warm bowl, sprinkle the yeast on the milk, and about ¾ cup of flour on top of the yeast - don't stir.

Cover the bowl, and set in a warm place until the flour and yeast sink. Make batter by adding the balance of the milk, egg yolks, and the remainder of the flour to the yeast mixture. Let the batter stand in a warm place for at least ½ hour before needed for cooking. Beat egg whites well and fold them into batter 10 minutes before cooking. Make 2 inch diameter cakes, frying them as you would ordinary pancakes.

Makes about 40 blini.

Serving Japanese Caviar

Please see Japanese Ingredients, chapter 24.

Japanese Red Caviar Appetizer

saki malt	red caviar
saki	

Steam sake malt; when cool, season with saki and mix with caviar. Refrigerate overnight before serving.

Caviar Salad

daikon (radish)	vinegar
caviar	light shoyu

Grate and drain radish.
Place caviar on bed of radish.
Sprinkle lightly with 2 parts vinegar, 1 part shoyu, garnish with parsley.

Taramasalata (creme salad) comes from Turkey and Greece. The original is made from grey mullet roe that has been salted, shaped like a sausage and dried.

Today because of the rareness and high cost of Tarama most Europeans, and Greeks, and Turks use smoked or canned cod roes. I find that any smoked or salted roe makes a wonderful taramasalata.

There are many recipes for making this creme salad and much diversity in the ingredients used; about the only thing they all have in common is the smoked or salted roe, lemon juice, and olive or corn oil.

If you are using smoked roe, no pre-processing is needed, but if using salted roe, soak it in fresh water for 1 to 2 hours depending on your taste for salt.

A mortar and pestle were originally used for the making, and still can be, but you will find that a blender takes the hard work out of taramasalata.

Ingredients

Basic: 4 oz. smoked or salted
    roes (Botargo)
1 tbs. to 12 oz. olive or
    corn oil
1 to 2 oz. lemon juice

Optional: 1 cup riced or mashed
    potatoes
3 oz. cream cheese
1 to 3 slices white bread
½ cup milk
3 oz. sour cream
1 tbs. chopped onion
1 tbs. chopped parsley
1 tbs. chopped chives
1 tsp. tomato puree
1 to 2 cloves garlic
black olives
capers

The base can be one of:
1. riced or mashed potatoes
2. white bread which has been decrusted and soaked in water or milk and squeezed out
3. cream cheese
4. sour cream

Put your choice in the blender along with the lemon juice and whatever of the flavorings you choose from:
1. onion
2. garlic
3. chives
4. tomato puree
5. parsley
6. black olives
7. capers

Gradually and alternately add to the blend pieces of roe and oil as you would in making mayonnaise. Sprinkle with parsley.

Serve the finished taramasalata with toast or in pastry sheels or in tartlets. Garnish with slices of black olives or capers.

Chapter **29**

Making Gravlax

Gravlax is a traditional Scandinavian salmon dish; originally *gravad lax* and apparently of Swedish origin. Now there are numerous different versions, including some from the continent as well as from Scandinavia.

In Scandinavia the salmon is usually prepared with more sugar than salt, lots of dill, and sometimes pine or spruce twigs. The amount of sugar and salt varies from country to country, (and from one practitioner to another), until in France salt dominates the sugar, and other fresh herbs completely replace the dill. The peppercorns used also vary. Some famous eating establishments insist that white peppercorns be freshly ground on the salmon; others accept the use of black while the most exotic recipe uses crushed, canned, green peppercorns.

Because of the growing scarcity of Atlantic salmon, Scandinavians often use the more abundant landlocked and sea run trout for this preparation. When trout are used the dish is known as Gravoring. For simplicity, I'll call the dish Gravlax whether made from salmon or trout.

How to Make Gravlax

Traditionally only the centre - cut of the fish is used because the two center - cut fillets can be reversed to *sandwich* closely together. Some dining places however, use the two complete fillets and simply weight the *sandwich* more to press the two together (see fig. 7).

Scandinavian Version

Sugar and salt can be varied to suit your taste - try these amounts to start. You can vary the ratio after the initial experience.

Per pound (0.5 kg) of fish

2 oz. (¼ cup) sugar (57 ml, 57 g)	1 oz. pickling salt (28 ml, 28 g)
freshly ground pepper	*4 oz. freshly chopped dill (112 g)
*pine, fir, hemlock twigs can be substituted for ½ of the dill.	

Dry dill weed can also be substituted for the fresh. If you're like us, you'll enjoy the dish all year round - not just when fresh dill is in season.

1. The traditional center-cut, the sugar-salt mix, fresh dill, and pepper ready for making Gravlax.

2. Sprinkle the alloted amount of sugar-salt mix over both pieces.

3. Grind fresh pepper (white or black) on the fish to suit your taste.

4. Cover one piece with the fresh chopped dill.

5. Place the second piece on the first, reversing its position so that the thick back part fits into the thin belly part of the first.

6. The *sandwich*, of the two pieces, can be on either a bed of chopped dill or pine, fir, etc. twigs.

7. Place a chopping board or similar on the sandwich, and weight it to press the 2 pieces together. You can do 2 sandwiches together, if you wish. If you do, put a layer of either dill or pine, etc. between the two sandwiches.

   Refrigerate.

Turn the sandwich of fish pieces over every 12 hours for 48 hours. Pour off juices that leach out.

Gravlax will keep at least 10 days under refrigeration.

SERVING GRAVLAX

8. Slice as thinly as possible in nearly a horizontal direction *toward the head* (or toward where the head used to be). This is important to get clean, unragged slices.

9. Wipe the knife off on a damp towel between slices; slicing is very difficult otherwise.

10. Traditional Gravlax service, for a fisherman's breakfast at dawn, or for any one at any time of the day - thin slices of Gravlax and cucumbers, served with buttered rye bread, Gravlax sauce, and thimbles of ice cold aquavit.

Gravlax Sauce

2 oz. vegetable oil (60 ml	2 tbs. minced fresh dill (36 ml)
1½ tbs. wine vinegar (27 ml)	

or

1 tsp. crushed dill weed (6 ml)	¼ tsp. salt (1.50 ml)
1 tbs. sugar (18 ml)	*3 tbs. prepared mustard (54 ml)

*Preferably a sweet - sour type of Swedish mustard.

Blend all ingredients including dried dill (but not fresh dill) together. If using fresh dill add it before serving.

Barbecued Gravlax

11. Gravlax is excellent barbecued over a smokey fire. Leave skin on the pieces, brush grill and fish with vegetable oil. A medium hot bed of coals (and smouldering wood) is best. Broil flesh side first and skin side last - neither will stick if fire is right. Broil about 10 minutes total (both sides) per inch of thickness - *don't over cook!*

CONTINENTAL GRAVLAX

Per pound (0.5 kg) of fish

1½ oz. pickling salt (27 ml)	freshly ground pepper
1 oz. sugar (18 ml)	*1 oz. chopped mixed herbs (18 ml)
2 tbs. cognac (36 ml)	

*Your choice of:

tarragon	fennel	parsley	shallots
thyme	basil	chervil	

12. After salt-sugar mix, and pepper have been sprinkled on fish pieces (see figs 2 & 3) chop and sprinkle on fresh herbs, and cognac. Then treat as in figs. 5,6 & 7.

    Refrigerate.

    Turn the sandwich of fish pieces over every 12 hours for 48 hours. Pour off juices that leach out.

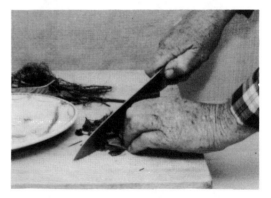

Serving Continental Gravlax

13. Dress individual servings with wine vinegar, olive oil, and *capers.

14. Sprinkle first the vinegar, then the oil, then capers over the slices.

15. Continental Gravlax ready to be served with buttered toast or buttered brown bread.

   *Homemade *capers*, as shown here, are excellent on this dish.

Homemade caper substitiute

Caper substitutes can come from you garden. Picking seedpods of the nasturtium for pickling.

Pickling formulas for seedpods

16 oz. white wine vinegar (480 ml)	¼ tsp. celery seed (1.5 ml)
1 tsp. pickling salt (6 ml)	2 peppercorns
¼ tsp. allspice (1.5 ml)	1 small onion, thinly sliced
¼ tsp. mace (1.5 ml)	

Simmer onion and spices in the vinegar-salt solution for 30 minutes, strain, and cool.

Put the half ripened seedpods in the spiced vinegar. They will keep for years in the refrigerator.

Chapter **30**

Fermented fish

I expect many of you to read this title with disbelief. Yet fermentation takes place in any *curing* process; it matters not whether it's fish, meat, milk, or soysauce. It's the *degree* of fermentation that makes a product acceptable to our noses and palates. For example, most people like mild cheddar cheese, but a lot of its admirers are lost as it ages or ripens, and most wouldn't even taste the same milk made into Camenbert or Limberger.

Cheese originated as a means of preserving milk in times of plenty (spring) for times when there was none to be had. Fish were fermented for the same reason, expecially in warm areas of the world with no natural means of *cooling*.

Anchovies are probably the best known example of fermented fish. They adorn millions of pizzas annually and more millions of salads and other dishes. Fermented fish, like cheese, come in different *strengths,* or stages of fermentation. Anchovies are about mid-range.

More for the novelty of its preparation than anything, I'll give a short description of some methods for preparing Fermented Fish.

Fermented fish liked by many peoples

This is not an uncommonly enjoyed fish product. The Romans made Garum from fermented fish, their entrails, and salt. It is said they could not do without if for flavoring.

There is still a fermented small fish product made in Italy called Pissalat which is used as a covering for Pissaladiera, a pizza like product.

Of course Southeast Asia is the largest user of fermented fish products in the form of nuoc-nam, patis, nuoc-cham, nam-pla, etc. These products used by millions daily, are a staple food.

The strength, purity, etc. is regulated by governement just as our milk is. It is a major source of readily digestible protein for children, again as milk is in North America.

Fermented Trout

Salted Fermented Small Trout are a Swedish delicacy that are a bit strong for the nose, of the uninitiated. Once past the nose and in the mouth, though, they're unusually flavorful.

For those who enjoy them and those who would like to try, here's how to make them:

Using equal weights of brine and fish, put the freshly caught, *uncleaned* fish in *saturated* brine, and stir them occassionally for the first few hours.

Take the fish out when the brine is diluted to 35° sal. (about 1½ days), and clean them. Leave roes in if you like.

Replace the fish in 70° sal. brine, being sure to *leave* some *headspace.* Cover with a loose fitting lid. You will know when the fish begin to ferment by the hydrogen sulfide gas (rotten egg). Because of the gas, you'll need some out of the way place to keep this ferment which is not designed to win friends.

The fermentation will take about 2 weeks; then the fish will have a new odor, like that used to odorate natural or bottled gas. Now put them in a closed container, *covered* and *submerged* in the same brine in which they were fermented.

Refrigerate the fermented fish for better keeping.

Yip Harm Yee

Hold uncleaned fish upright and pour salt in mouth pushing salt down with chopstick or similar utensil to fill the body cavity. Rub salt well into gills and around head. Lay fish flat; weight with stone or other suitable weight, and leave overnight.

Next day wrap fish in brown paper, tie with string and hang in sun 2 or 3 days.

Clean fish, cut into pieces, place in shallow bowl, sprinkle with shredded green ginger and vegetable oil, steam for 20 minutes. Serve small portions

Koessed Heids

Wind Blawn Fish

with plain boiled rice as an appetizer or, steam fish with equal amount of minced or ground pork which has been seasoned with salt, and sugar. Sprinkle fish and pork with shredded green ginger and vegetable oil, steam 20 to 25 minutes.

Koessed Heids

The Shetland Isles have another example of slightly fermented fish: Koessed Heids. The directions call for the use of a hole in a stone wall for the fermentation, a requisite not generally available; presumably any cool place would do.

To make Koessed Heids, lightly salt salmon or trout heads and wrap them in a cloth or stout paper. Keep them in a cool place until they get suitably gamey for your taste, then roast them.

Blawn Fish

Scotland has probably the simplest fermentation - process: *Blawn* or Wind Blown. It truly is more of a conditioning than a fermentation, because there is no noticeable change in flavor, rather, an intensification of flavor.

To make Blawn fish, clean, skin, and remove eyes from *freshly caught* trout or salmon up to 1 lb. in weight. Cover, and fill the body cavity with salt, then immediately shake off as much of the salt as possible. Hang the salted fish in a cool breezy place at least 8 hours.

Without any wiping or rinsing, flour the fish, and depending on size and your preference, either fry them in butter or broil and serve, dressed with butter.

Sun Drenched Salmon or Trout

Sprinkle salmon fillets liberally with salt and refrigerate for 24 hours.

Season with freshly ground pepper and oregano, cover with cheese cloth and place in a sunny, breezy spot until firm and a little dry (about 3 hours).

Brush with olive oil and grill over charcoal, or in oven, for 10 minutes per inch (25 mm) of thickness, turning at half time.

This process gives a slightly more cured flavor than wind blown.

5

FREEZING & CANNING

CONTENTS

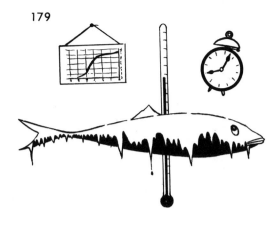

Chapter **31**

Fish - a special
freezing problem

In the thirty five years that I have owned a home freezer, I have read everything I could find on freezing fish at home. Neither the popular press, cookbook publishers, home economists, nor government agencies, told me the most important freezing fact: that home freezers *aren't good for freezing fish.* They're fine for *keeping* frozen fish, but *not for freezing.* I'll explain this provocative statement, and more importantly, tell what you can do about it.

Fish a special freezing problem

Fish present a complex freezing problem. For that reason, any but the very best freezing process yields only a fair to poor product. I consistantly hear people complain about the quality of their home frozen fish, and for that reason, they throw out much potentially nutritious food every year. I am even amazed to find that a considerable proportion of the commercially frozen fish, expecially that from small commercial establishments, is badly frozen. What, then, constitutes *good* fish freezing?

Good fish freezing gets much study

Food scientists in many countries, devote much effort toward making fish more palatable and nutritious for the consumer. This is especially so in countries where fish are a more important source of protein that they are here in North America. Some countries where fish as food has received lots of attention are: Great Britain, Russia, Japan, and Germany. There are many translations of non-English language reports, but the bulk of the fish processing data, available to us who read English only, comes from Great Britain. I am impressed with the very complete studies on fish, the English food scientists have done and with how well the information is disseminated to the commercial fishermen and the fish trade.

These scientists have studied freezing thoroughly because freezing *can* keep the nutritive value of fish high and yet keep the fish as close to fresh tasting as possible.

Quick freezing definition

Great Britain is so aware of the necessity for freezing fish quickly, that *Quick Freezing* has been standardized by government. *"Quick Freezing* is a process whereby the whole of the fish is reduced in temperature from 32° F (0° C) to 23° F (-5° C) in *not more than 2 hours,* and the fish is retained in the freezer until the warmest part is reduced to -5° F (-20° C) or lower," according to the Ministry of Agriculture, Fisheries, and Food.

Taste panel tests have proven that if freezing to 23° F takes longer than *4 hours,* the results begin to be noticeable in loss or change of flavor from fresh.

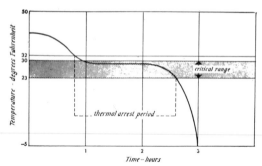

Ideal freezing curve for fish muscle

Why quick freezing is difficult

The freezing zone between 32° F and 23° F is specified because in that zone the fish is most difficult to freeze. In this zone, known as the thermal arrest period, water in the fish starts freezing at about 30° F, as the water changes state - turns to ice - a tremendous amount of heat is given off, and must be removed by the refrigerating system. Also, as water freezes, minerals, etc. that are dissolved in the water, are left in the remaining unfrozen water.

In other words the solution of minerals, protein, etc. gets stronger because the water freezes but the dissolved ingredients don't, (anti-freeze effect). So, as more water freezes out, the concentrated mineral solution becomes more and more resistant to freezing.

Slow freezing ruins fish quality

This concentrated mineral solution, if slowly frozen will result in large ice crystals which damage the fragile connective tissue in fish muscle. This tissue damage becomes evident in thawing, with increased loss of moisture from the fish. This lost moisture (known as "drip" in the fish trade) carries away from the fish much of its flavor and succulence making poorly frozen fish taste, one discriminating critic said, "Like a cooked, salted and peppered

brown paper bag." During this time of difficult freezing, caused by the anti-freeze effect of the concentrated minerals, you must have a *good* refrigeration system capable of freezing the fish quickly in spite of the concentrated minerals. Then, the quality of the fish when thawed will be indistinguishable from fresh.

There is a further problem caused by concentration of soluble ingredients, in the body water of the fish, during freezing. In addition to minerals. there are proteins dissolved in the body water. Some of these proteins are enzymes (the Spoilers) talked about back in chapter 1. The enzymes continue to break down the fish even at temperatures below 32° F. If you freeze fish slowly, as the water gradually freezes, the spoiling enzymes are being concentrated - getting stronger and stronger - and are working harder to spoil the fish.

They are spoiling faster than you are stopping their action by cooling. As a result of slow freezing, fish will not only be dry and tasteless, it will also have undesirable, spoiled flavors.

How fish is frozen

First of all, to cool and then freeze anything you must *remove heat* from it, as you may remember from school days: "There is no such thing as cold; there is only heat - more heat, or less heat." So if you remove enough heat from food, it will freeze. In cooling, ice, or the cooling coils in the refrigerator, take the heat from the air and the cold air then takes the heat from warmer food. Once the food is cool, then only the heat coming through the walls of the refrigerator must be carried away by the ice or the cooling coils. The heat is disposed of, in the case of ice, by the ice melting and the water running away. A mechanical refrigerator disposes of the heat, which its cooling coils accept, by carrying it to other coils outside the box, which in turn dispose of the heat to the outside air.

To freeze food or anything else, the system for carrying away heat must simply operate at a lower temperature range - low enough to reduce the temperature to below freezing.

How a good commercial freezer works

Here's how a well designed and well operated commercial plant freezes fish:

The refrigerating coils would be cold, about -30° F (-35° c) or colder.

The freezing would be done in a tunnel where the air was moving at about 1,000 feet a minute to carry the heat away from the fish to the refrigerating coils. The air would be bathing all the fish evenly so they would all freeze at the same rate.

If the plant were not the *air blast* type, as discribed above, it would probably be a plate freezer. The refrigerant would be pumped through hollow plates and the fish placed between the plates. In the better plants a single layer of fish or thin packages of fish are *sandwiched* between two plates by slight hydraulic pressure so the contact will be good, and the freezing fast; of course the plant will have many such *sandwiches.*

Home freezing vs. commercial freezing

Now how does the home freezer compare with excellent commercial freezers? We have two chest-type freezers because of our self sufficient life style. The best of the two, operates at a *low* of -10° F the other about -5° F. In our nearly new refrigerator the freezer runs between 0° F and 10° F at the *lowest* setting. So at home we start at a disadvantage with higher freezer temperatures and consequent lower freezing potential.

How a home freezer freezes

How does the cooling get done in a home freezer? How does the heat get from the fish to the refrigerating system? In that respect our new refrigerator freezer is the best system in our house, because it has a circulating fan in the freezer compartment which carries heat directly to frost-free refrigerating coils (I'll talk about that later). One of our chest freezers has a *freezing* compartment with refrigerating coils on the bottom. Food to be frozen can be laid in contact with the bottom for better heat conductivity to the refrigerating coils. At best, however, the coils are only on one side of the fish, so heat must pass all the way through the fish to get to the coils on the bottom. The second freezer has its refrigerating coils in the walls of the cabinet. For food to freeze, air must carry heat from it to the walls. The problem with this system is that the air doesn't move very much, and if the freezer is nearly full, there's not much bare wall to accept the heat. What really happens is that the other food in the freezer must accept the heat. This is especially so it you put a fan in the freezer. The faster moving air can't get to the coils in the wall because they are either covered by food packages or by ice (frost) which insulates them nicely. So the already frozen food accepts the heat from the newly added food and up goes the temperature of the stored food. If we are constantly adding *new* food, the temperature of the *stored* food is going up and down like a busy elevator—thawing and freezing—thawing and freezing. The enzymes in the food are warmed up enough to go to work spoiling, then slowed, then again speeded up—ad infinitum!

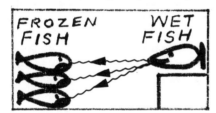

Effects of freezing fish on stored frozen fish

Tests in commercial fish plants show that if wet (unfrozen) fish is added to stored frozen fish, *5 lbs.* of wet fish will raise the temperature of *100 lbs.* of frozen fish by *14°F.*

To further give you an idea of what a refrigeration load wet fish imposes on a freezing system: 1 ton of frozen fish can be *stored* at -20° F with only a *½ h.p.* refrigeration plant, but to *freeze* 1 ton of wet fish to -20° F in 2 hours takes a *50 h.p.* plant.

To freeze 1 ton fish in 2 hours at -20° F

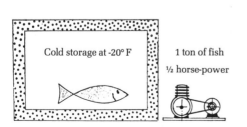

Cold storage at -20° F

1 ton of fish
½ horse-power

50 horse-power

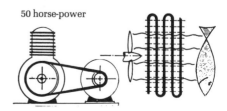

Recap of home freezing problems

Here is a recap of the difficulties of doing a good job of freezing fish at home before going on to a solution to the problem.

1.   Refrigeration units on home freezers are only large enough to *keep* food frozen after it has *been* frozen. Small amounts of food 5% of freezer capacity)—other than wet fish—can adequately be frozen at home. This includes *smoked* fish.

2.   Home freezers, as usually used, do not have a good means of getting heat from wet fish to the refrigeration coils for removal.

3.   Wet fish should not be frozen in the same space with stored frozen fish. The stored fish will suffer by absorbing heat from the wet unfrozen fish.

Test results in home freezers

The enumerated shortcomings of our home freezers aren't simply some impractical foreign scientists' opinions. I have been measuring them in my equipment for the last 7 years and have gone so far as to build my own portable freezer for my camper. In measuring the inadequacies of a home freezer for freezing fish I have used our best freezer which has a larger refrigeration unit than most. Here are my findings:

1.   Advice that comes with home freezers, and from home economists, tells me not to try to freeze more than 10% of the carrying capacity of the freezer (in pounds of food). 5% is said to be a more practical figure.

When I froze 5% of the capacity, the temperature of all the stored food rose from -6° F to 14° F and stayed there until the newly added fish was nearly frozen. Tests show that enzymes in the fish do their destructive work *8 time faster* at 14° F than they do at ideal storage temperature.

2.   When I froze even small amounts of fish, in a freezer with a *deep freeze* compartment, in water in a container *smaller* that the often-used milk carton, it took *13 hours* to get to 23° F. As shown earlier, the ideal time to do this is *2 hours* (see Quick Freezing Defined).

How to cure home freezing problems

What to do about it? Don't throw your hands up in despair and stop freezing fish. Make the best of a difficult situation:

1.   Buy a thermometer that will let you know what is happening inside your freezer. They are readily available at your hardware store.

2.   Your *refrigerator* undoubtedly has a freezing compartment - it's almost impossible to buy one without - If it has a circulating fan, use it to *freeze* your fish. But be sure to remove any *stored* frozen fish first; move it to your *storage* freezer.

3.   No matter what kind of freezer you have, keep the refrigerating coils clear as much as possible. If the coils are on the inside walls, keep them clear of frost, if there are coils on the bottom of a compartment, or in one or more shelves, keep them clear of frost.

Keep the upper part of chest freezer walls clear of food. Baskets that hold frozen food should allow easy access of air to the walls.

Chapter **32**

How to improve home freezing

I have pointed out how the *stored food*, in a home freezer, absorbs the heat from wet fish - the stored food becomes a *heat sink* because the refrigerating system can't absorb the heat fast enough. The stored food later gradually dissipates the heat to the refrigerating system. You have seen that this warming is detrimental to the stored food, but also the stored food is a poor heat acceptor. The stored food is only frozen water and water ice doesn't have much ability to accept heat until it reaches the thawing point at around 32° F (0° C).

My solution for freezing problems

I have worked out a solution to the problem by adding a separate heat sink to the freezer, that allows me to **slowly store quick freezing capacity** for times when I want to freeze wet fish. How is this possible? I use a special solution that freezes (and thaws) at about 0° F (-17° C) - unlike water which freezes and thaws at 32° F (0° C). This *special* ice, like water ice, absorbs an unusually large amount of heat *when it melts,* but it keeps its surroundings at around 0° F (-17° C) while it melts.

Storing freezing capacity

You can see, then, that by having all this heat absorbing ability stored, waiting for me to catch some fish, I can do a superb job of freezing them when I do. The special *heat sink* can quickly absorb the heat from the wet fish, keeping their quality high, and yet not impair the quality of the stored fish. The refrigerating system can then *gradually* absorb the captured heat from the *heat sink.*

Heat sink ready for freezing fish

Heat sink helps in emergency

A fringe benefit from having a separate heat sink in the freezer, especially one with such a low melting point, comes if the freezer goes off for any reason. When you have a power or mechanical failure, the food temperature quickly rises to around 32° F (0° C) and stays there until the food completely thaws. The food may feel frozen to the touch but the damage is done - to fish especially. If the freezer again begins to function, the fish *slowly* freezes and its quality is damaged. Frozen fish that has warmed to 32° F should be eaten, canned, smoked or otherwise processed. A separate, low melting heat sink in the freezer allieviates the problem of the fish warming, by keeping the temperature near 0° F (-18° C) for an extended time.

Heat sink good for transporting frozen fish

The special heat sink has another valuable use too; it allows me to transport frozen fish without having to find and buy expensive dry ice. True, it takes more of the special ice than dry ice, because its temperature is higher than dry ice, but it's virtually free - just the cost of refreezing. It's mighty handy to be able to take *specialties,* like frozen smoked fish, etc., to our distant families when we visit. Two or three days en route is no problem with a well insulated container and the special ice.

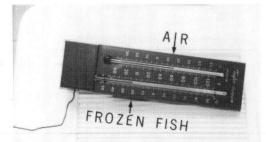

Heat sink excellent for transporting frozen fish

How to make the special ice heat sink

The *special ice* that absorbs large amounts of heat when it melts, at around 0° F (-18° C) instead of at 32° F (0° C) as regular ice does, is called a *eutectic* solution. There are 2 different eutectic solutions useful in home freezing. One is cheaper than the other and thaws at a lower temperature. The one you can use will depend on the lowest temperature your freezer will reach, so first find your *minimum* temperature.

The cheapest and coldest eutectic solution is made from common salt - sodium chloride. The solution must have a precise make-up to work.

Sodium chloride (pickling salt) eutectic solution formula

Pickling salt	23% by weight
Water	77% by weight

Sodium chloride eutectic solution *will not* freeze unless your freezer is colder than -6° F (-21° C) and even then it freezes very slowly in a home freezer. Even small containers will take about a week to freeze, but that is also an advantage. The slow freezing automatically regulates the load on the freezer and its contents.

If your freezer won't go down to -6° F (-21° C) but will get down to 2° F (-17° C) you can make a different eutectic solution, that will freeze and thaw at 2° F, from ammonium nitrate fertilizer.

Ammonium nitrate eutectic solution formula

Ammonium nitrate	42% by weight
Water	58% by weight

You can find ammonium nitrate at garden or farm supply stores.

Either of the eutectic solutions will absorb heat better if contained in metal. They both, however will corrode metal, so you may want to sacrifice some of the heat transfer ability of the metal for the longevity of glass or plastic containers.

Ammonium nitrate is *not* a food item, so you will naturally want to keep it from contacting food.

Each time your eutectic solution melts, stir or shake to be sure that any salt, thrown out of solution, is redissolved before refreezing.

Using a Heat Sink for Quick Freezing

If the *heat sink* I talk about is to freeze fish quickly there must be some efficient way to move heat from the fish into the *heat sink*. Moving heat by air is not efficient. Air can carry so relatively little heat, that lots of it must be used to freeze quickly. For example, commercial blast freezers use air moving at 1,000 ft. a minute or faster - a feat that's nearly impossible at home unless you build a special freezer.

Cold brine efficient freezer

One of the most efficient ways of freezing fish is to immerse it in a salt brine. Salt brine doesn't freeze solid until it gets down to -6° F (-22° C) and then only slowly. Fish immersed in cold brine freeze quickly and efficiently because the brine is an excellent conductor to carry heat from the fish to a heat sink immersed in the brine. This method was widely used in the past, especially at sea, but the fish absorbed too much salt while freezing. The absorbed salt put consumers off and also lessened the keeping quality of fat fish. As a result, brine freezing is *little* used today.

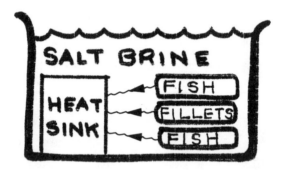

Poly bag protects fish from salt brine

At home, however, I can brine freeze without getting salt in the fish, by placing the fish in a *thin poly freezer bag*. The *thin* bag does not hinder heat transfer measurably! With the heat sink, and its stored-up ability to absorb heat, in the brine with the fish. I get double quick freezing!

Fish fillets will *quick freeze* in *1 hour!*

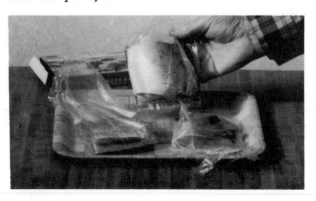

Brine freezing has other benefits

Another benefit I get from brine freezing comes from the pressure of the brine on the bags, pushing out virtually all the trapped air - air that would oxidize the fish and cause rancidity. *After* the fish is quickly frozen, I add a *small* amount of water to the bags to fill any minute air spaces that might be left. The small amount of water needed affects fish temperature very little; a temperature measuring probe in the center of the fish recorded only change of 2° F while the added water froze.

Stout rubber bands make a *jacket* around the fish which excludes air, minimizes the skin of water, then ice around the frozen fish.

HOW TO MAKE A EUTECTIC ICE-BRINE FREEZER

A simple brine tank, able to freeze 8 lbs. of fillets, made from a plastic dishpan. This will give you ideas for making your own.

Slotted strips hold bagged fish in place.

Solid strips retain eutectic ice; strips can be plexiglas or plywood. Drink cans, sealed with duct tape hold eutectic ice.

Double-bagged fillets slip into slotted strips.

Clothes pins hold bags in place.

Bag-holding strips slip into wire retaining loops.

Pouring -6° F brine into loaded tank. Brine forces air from bags of fish. The filled tank then goes into your home freezer.

COMPARING METHODS OF FREEZING

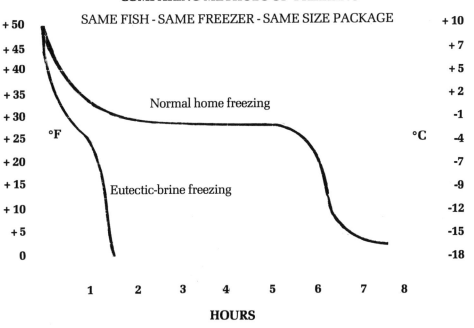

SAME FISH - SAME FREEZER - SAME SIZE PACKAGE

Normal home freezing

°F   °C

Eutectic-brine freezing

HOURS

Chapter **33**

Other freezing considerations

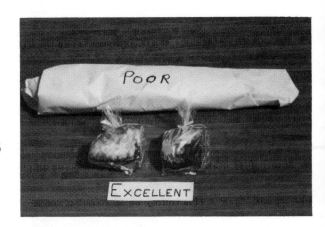

POOR

EXCELLENT

Fish size important in freezing

Since the key to keeping the *fresh quality* in fish, during freezing, is *quick freezing,* anything that *slows down* freezing should be avoided. Thickness affects quick freezing. Naturally, the freezing of fish must start at the outside and proceed in toward the center. Fish flesh is a poor conductor of heat, so the thicker the fish the more difficult it is to remove the heat from the center. I realize that the effect of thickness on freezing is easily understood logic, but I think it is worth dwelling on for a minute.

Those who freeze fish commercially and find it *necessary* to freeze fish *whole,* have a problem if they wish to *quick freeze* - (See Quick Freezing Defined). Even at the extremely low freezing temperature of -40° F (-40°C), *in an efficient blast* or *plate* freezer, a fish thickness of 7 in. (175 mm) is the most that can be *quick frozen* in 4 hours. Think of the contrast between those ideal freezing conditions and the conditions that normally exist in our home freezers. I find that the home freezer, under average conditions, takes *5½ hours* to cool a *1 in. (25 mm)* fillet to 23° F, instead of the 2 to 4 hours desired; and that fillet was covered only with a 1 mil poly bag. Fish frozen in water take as long as 13 hours.

Obviously, the thing to do with thick fish is to reduce its thickness for quick freezing. Unfortunately, I see more fish, caught at fish camps, frozen in the round - usually with only head and tail removed. I can understand that some people enjoy a whole baked or poached fish for serving to a large gathering.

If you wish to serve a fish in this way, use only a fresh, unfrozen fish because a whole fish can *not* be successfully *quick frozen* in the home freezer.

At our home, we enjoy cooking fish many ways, but enjoy most fish cooked briefly over a smokey fire - outdoors in good weather or indoors in our fireplace. But regardless of how we use the fish, serving-size pieces of fillets are handiest.

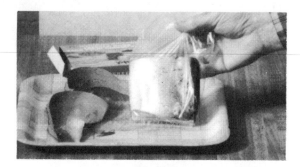

Using the methods in chapter 3, a 5 lb. (2 kg) fish can be filleted in 2 or 3 minutes (if scaled and cleaned first). I then cut the fillets into individual pieces for serving 1 person. I most often pack 2 serving pieces in a 1 pint size freezer bag, with the skin side out, and the pieces facing thick end to thin end. If two fillets, thus packed, exceed 1½ in. (39 mm) in thickness (which seldom occurs with the fish I catch) I pack the fillets separately. Even with my improved freezing method (see using a Heat Sink for Quick Freezing) a 1½ in. thick package is all that will perfectly quick freeze. Steaks of course, can also be handled this way, and extremely thick fillets can be cut lengthwise into thinner ones.

Storing Frozen Fish

I'm sure that everyone knows that it is necessary to protect frozen fish in storage from the air, but I'm not sure that everyone fully knows why and how.

The *why* has 2 reasons, especially since you are concerned with trout and salmon - fatty fish:

1. The fish must be protected against evaporation of moisture from its surface - i.e. drying - *freezer burn.* Evaporation goes on just as surely at 0° F as it does at 100° F; it's just slower at low temperature. That's where much of the frost on the inside of freezer walls or on refrigerating coils comes from, or if your unit is frost free, the water in the drip pan came partially from evaporation off the food. So cover the food you must to prevent *drying*.

2. The fat in trout and salmon reacts with oxygen in the air to cause the rancidity that ruins flavor. Commercial testing has found *no* means of preventing oxidation other than excluding air. So cover the food you must to prevent *rancidity*.

The *how* of protecting frozen fish is most important, because if it's poorly done you are living in a *fool's paradise*, thinking that your precious fish is well looked after, when in effect it is only slightly if at all protected. Why so? The fish may be wrapped up along with a lot of air; air in spaces in and around the fish. While the wrap may cover the fish, outside air may still have access through folds or tears in the wrapping. Just wrapping, then, is poor protection.

Glazing best protection

The best way yet found by the Fish Packing Industry to protect frozen fish in storage, is with a *covering of ice* - (a glazing of ice). Often sportsmen at home go beyound the glazing, and freeze fish in a block. If you freeze fish in a block of ice, you are adding more of a freezing load to the system and in doing that, you are affecting the freezing *rate* of the fish. Get the fish frozen as soon as possible, and protect it later. Remember that the rate of freezing greatly influences the eating quality of the fish. Glazing by dipping or spraying later will have little or no effect on quality.

Glazing also needs protection

Even glazed fish still require some care however. The ice of the glaze is also subject to evaporation; it will eventually disappear just as ice cubes do in your refrigerator if not used. You can reglaze the fish from time to time, but the best solution is one I saw while researching commercial smoking.

In Scotland I saw frozen Pacific Salmon, that had been expensively imported for smoking. They were not only heavily glazed, but were also *sealed* in heavy poly bags to prevent evaporation. Your fish deserve the same care.

Glazing doubly important for smoked fish

Salmon and trout are usually fat fish, and part of the smoking process includes salting. Salt causes fat to oxidize much faster than it ordinarily would, so it is extremely important to protect fat, smoked fish from the air. Glaze smoked fish just as you would fresh, then protect the glaze from evaporating.

Thawing Frozen Fish

This may seem to be a subject that is unworthy of discussion, but since I'm always shooting for fresh-like quality in frozen fish, proper thawing is important.

Thawing in water is the simplest, and is excellent for whole fish. Caution is necessary, however, when you thaw *fillets* in water. Fillets left in water too long can easily get waterlogged and lose considerable flavor. Fatter fillets can stand more water immersion than thin ones, but they too will eventually become waterlogged.

My system for freezing fillets in small blocks in freezer bags, (as described in chapter 32) lends itself to thawing in water without waterlogging. Since the bags in which the fillets were frozen are seldom watertight after being handled while stored in the freezer, my first move when thawing a block of fillets is to remove the bag - tear it off.

Secondly, I put the block in tepid water for a few minutes to melt away the small skin of ice around the fillets.

Lastly, I take the block out of the water, let it drain briefly, *then carefully* place it in a new freezer bag, and return it to the water. This gives excellent heat transfer from the warmer water to thaw the fish without its getting waterlogged.

If you have frozen your fish in containers of water, you can also thaw in air to avoid waterlogging, but if you do, first remove the fish from any container it may be in and set it on a rack so that the covering ice can drain away from the fish as it melts.

Another caution about thawing in air; it is usually much slower than water thawing, and if speeded up by moving air (fan or breeze) the fish may dry out and loose succulence and flavor.

Chapter **34**

What you
must know
about canning

The home canning of salmon and trout is a subject that cookbooks, and books on preserving food for home use, generally refuse to discuss. Readers are told to consult government agencies for correct canning procedures. Some government agencies have no formal statement to make on the subject; they try to discourage home canning of fish, because of the possible hazards involved. But I don't find this realistic, or in the best interests of the public, because I see most fishermen I know, canning fish. People are going to can even if they have to use *poor advice* from another fisherman, and there is plenty of poor advice being freely given, I find. I believe that anyone interested in fish canning should know how to can properly, and clearly understand the *extreme hazard* of *not* following the rules down to the *smallest* detail. I hope these chapters will accomplish that goal.

Why all this fuss about home canning fish? *Improperly* canned fish (as well as other food), can carry botulism - a deadly poison. What is botulism? Here is a brief discussion of botulism contained in Leaflet 2425 of the Cooperative Extension service, U.S. Department of Agriculture, University of California, "Canning and Freezing Fish at Home."

• Beware of Botulism

If you do not carefully and completely follow the directions given in this publication, or if you have any doubts about the contents of a jar or can, do not taste the food. Boil home-canned products for at least 10 minutes. This applies to all home-canned, low-acid foods—vegetables (including those canned in acid), meats, poultry, and fish. Acid foods, such as fruits, tomatoes, rhubarb, and pickles, may become low acid through the growth of mold.

A form of food poisoning called botulism is caused by the toxin produced when botulinum bacteria are present. These bacteria grow in the absence of air in foods that are low in acid or that have become low acid. The toxin is one of the most poisonous substances known. However, it can be completely destroyed by boiling. Never taste food that appears to be spoiled. •

Following is a more complete discussion of botulism contained in a dispatch from the Health Protection Branch of <u>Health and Welfare Canada.</u>

●No 41
Date Summer 1976

Botulism and Home Canning

In Canada last year, four people died after eating improperly prepared marine products. They were victims of the deadliest form of food poisoning known to man, BOTULISM. Though it is extremely rare, botulism strikes several Canadians every year. There have been a few cases of botulism due to inadequately processed commercially prepared foods, but most outbreaks are associated with home prepared foods which have been improperly preserved, stored under anaerobic (in the absence of oxygen) conditions, and consumed without appropriate heating.

What is Botulism?

Botulism is a food-borne illness or food intoxication caused by the spore-forming microorganism, Clostridium botulinum. This bacteria and its spores are found everywhere; in the soil, on raw fruits and vegetables, and on meat and fish. The spores are the inactive form of the bacteria and are very resistant to adverse conditions, such as heat and chemical treatment, that normally will destroy the actively growing micro-organism. However, in low-acid food, under anaerobic conditions, the botulinum spores become active, begin to grow, and product a toxin or poisonous substance. If a food becomes contaminated and is eaten without sufficient heat treatment to destroy the toxin, severe illness and, in many cases, death can occur.

Botulism is a tragic and poorly understood disease. It differs from other types of bacterial-caused food poisoning, in that it affects the nervous system rather than the digestive tract.

How does it occur?

Botulinum toxin can occur in low-acid canned or processed foods whenever inadequate heating or processing permits spore survival. Conditions which contribute to the development of toxin are:

- lack of air, as in a sealed can, jar, or plastic package;
- foods which contain little or no added acid: some examples are meat, poultry, fish, seafood, mushrooms, eggs and most vegetables; chili peppers, cucumbers and certain varieties of tomatoes have only a medium acid content and should be treated with care;
- temperatures between 4°C (40°F) and 46°C (115°F). Growth of the spores is fastest at about 38°C (100°F).

If these conditions are present and adequate precautions are not taken, botulinum spores can germinate and produce a toxin so potent that one cupful of the pure toxin, it is estimated, could kill the entire population of the world.

Sometimes cans or jars with food containing botulinum toxin will bulge or have off odours, but this doesn't always happen. It is not uncommon for a botulinum-contaminated food to appear and smell normal.

Frozen or dried foods and those with high concentreations of acid, salt or sugar do not support the growth of botulinum bacteria.

Symptoms of Botulism Poisoning

The early signs of botulism—fatigue, weakness and blurred vision—usually develop about 8 to 72 hours after eating food containing botulinum toxin. These symptoms are followed by laboured breathing, difficulty in speaking clearly, dizziness, headaches, abdominal discomfort, vomiting and muscle paralysis. Botulism is difficult to diagnose because of its rare occurrence and the similarity of its symptoms to many other illnesses. An antitoxin does exist, but it should be given as soon as possible and is not always completely effective.

Health Protection Branch Control

Under the authority of the Food and Drugs Act and Regulations, the Health Protection Branch of the Department of National Health and Welfare regulates the manufacture and distribution of food products sold in Canada. General provisions in the Act make it possible for the Branch to exercise control over the spread of pathogenic micro-organisms. Several regulations deal specifically with the problem of C. botulinum. Some examples are:

- Fish - smoked fish or smoked fish products which are packed in containers sealed to exclude air must be heat processed after sealing at a temperature and for a time sufficient to destroy C. botulinum.
- Meat - meats packed in hermetically sealed containers must be heat processed to prevent the survival of any toxin-producing micro-organisms. Meats which are not heat treated in this way must be subjected to further processing such as freezing, dehydration, or the addition of preservatives or an acid medium.

In addition to legislation the Health Protection Branch plays a major role in inspection, research and education to ensure a safe food supply for Canadians.

Botulism Reference Centre

Recently, the work of the Botulism Reference Centre for Canada has come under the responsibility of the Health Protection Branch. This Centre provides several important services such as investigating cases of food poisoning where botulism is suspected, alerting responsible agencies when a commercially produced food is involved, accumulating information on botulism, and maintaining reference cultures and supplies of antitoxin.

Whenever botulism is suspected, you should contact your physician or local health unit immediately so that they can alert the Botulism Reference Centre, and if necessary commence treatment.

Preventive Measures for Consumers

As a consumer, food safety in the home is YOUR responsibility. To guard against botulism, follow these simple preventive guidelines:

Commercially Prepared Foods

- Never use or even taste canned foods that show any sign of spoilage. Bulging can ends and jar lids usually indicate spoilage. When you open the container, check for off odours, froth, foam or mould.
- When a commercially prepared food is involved, a large number of people may be at risk; therefore, report any suspect food to your local public health authorities or the Health Protection Branch.

Home Canned Foods

- Always follow recommended canning procedures (See NOTE).
- All vegetables, meat, and fish must be processed in a pressure canner. Boiling temperatures are insufficient to destroy all the bacterial spores in these foods. Meat and fish are particularly susceptible to the growth of botulinum bacteria; they are not recommended for home canning.
- Check containers and contents before using the food. If there are any signs of spoilage, do not taste it. **THROW IT OUT.**
- Often there may be no signs of spoilage. As an extra measure of safety, it is a wise precaution to boil home canned vegetables for 10 minutes before tasting.
- A reminder: canned fruits, jams and jellies, and pickles and relishes do not cause botulism; high concentrations of acid, salt or sugar prevent the growth of botulinum bacteria.

  NOTE: Agriculture Canada's booklet "Canning Canadian Fruits and Vegetables", No. 1560 may be obtained by writing the Information Division, Agriculture Canada, Ottawa K1A 0C7 ●

Authors note: Safe canning times from both Fisheries and Oceans, Canada, and The United States Department of Agriculture are given in chapter 35.

Great Britain, too, has done considerable research on botulism and the Torry Research Station, of the Ministry of Agriculture, Fisheries and Food,

Aberdeen, Scotland has issued a report on the subject: The report doesn't concern canned fish but discusses smoked fish that has been vacuum packed. (Note that the Canadian report also is concerned with "Smoked fish or smoked fish products that are packed *in containers* sealed to exclude air –"). The Torry report is quoted in part:

• What is botulism?

Botulism is an often fatal food poisoning disease caused by one of the most powerful toxins known to man. A toxin is a poison produced by certain bacteria when they grow on food; the king of bacterium that forms the toxin causing botulism is called *Clostridium botulinum.* When food containing the toxin is eaten, the nervous system is affected and death can follow within hours.

Clostridium Botulinum in Fish

There are seven known types of *Clostridium botulinum,* referred to as types A-G; of these, A, B, E and F consistently produce botulism in humans, and B, E and F are frequently found in the sea.

Authentic cases of botulism have been recorded in recent years in places as far apart as Japan, Scandinavia and North America. Since these have been due mainly to type E, usually in association with the eating of seafoods of various kinds, worldwide attention has been given to the occurrence of type E in fish and fishery products.

Clostridium botulinum grows only in the absence of oxygen, and type E, and some varieties of B and F, have two important properties. First, they are found in fish intestines and gills and in mud from the sea, whereas the other types are found mostly in soil. Secondly, they grow and form toxin at a much lower temperature than the other types; they can grow at $5°C$ in fish products. Fortunately the toxin is readily destroyed by cooking since it does not survive exposure to $70°C$ for 2 minutes.

Smoked fish and botulism

Many of the salmon and trout that are smoked in this country are imported from Japan, Denmark and the Pacific coast of North America. *Clostridium botulinum* type E has been found in all these areas of the world. Moreover, sliced smoked salmon is sold in quantity in vacuum packs.

Salmon flesh is either dry salted or brined before being cold smoked, the time of salting varying with the size of salmon being cured. The presence of salt in the product has a great effect on the growth of *Clostridium botulinum,* but the concentration of salt in smoked salmon is not usually high enough to prevent growth altogether; commercial smoked salmon usually contains 1 to 4 per cent salt. The concentration required to prevent growth at room temperature can vary from as low as 3½ per cent to 5 per cent or more, so that the amount of salt present in smoked salmon is on its own no guarantee against the danger of botulism.

Trout and mackerel are brined and then hot smoked, either as gutted whole fish or as fillets. The range of salt concentration is similar to that found in salmon. Details of the smoking process for salmon, mackerel and trout are given in Advisory Notes 5, 66 and 74 respectively. Since neither the smoking not the drying parts of present processes are particularly severe, *Clostridium botulinum* can survive and flourish in the finished product, unless it is kept sufficiently cool.

How to control botulism

Before the toxin of *Clostridium botulinum* can develop in a fishery product a number of factors must coincide: the organism must be present in the fish, the time and temperature of storage must be favourable for toxin production, and the chemical composition of the product must be such that it supports the growth of the organism. *Elimination of any one of these factors will make the product safe.*

In practice it is not possible to rid a contaminated fish of botulinum organisms but removal of the guts and gills, followed by thorough washing of the belly cavity with tap water, can reduce contamination by as much as 90 per cent.

Starvation of farmed trout for 1 - 3 days before harvesting is beneficial as fish with empty guts cause less contamination during processing. For this procedure to be effective, however, the starved fish should be held in concrete or plastics ponds; hungry trout in dirt ponds will feed off the contaminated mud.

Clostridium botulinum types B, E and F can grow and produce toxin at 5°C in some fish products; the lowest recorded temperature for growth in any food is 3.3°C, when the product took 31 days to become toxic. *In practice, therefore, if fish are adequately iced immediately after catching and kept below 4°C at all stages of processing until eaten, they will remain safe.*

Caterers and retailers receiving deliveries of fresh fish must inspect and where necessary re-ice them to maintain the temperature of the fish below 4°C. Where the amount of ice on receipt is insufficient, the supplier should be notified. A chillroom operating at 4°C can be used to conserve ice around fish but cannot be used satisfactorily to cool uniced fish or keep them cool. Packaged fish should carry a 'Sell by ......' date according to the type of product, clearly marked 'Store below 4°C' and carry a recommendation that the contents be eaten within 24 hours if kept at room temperature and within 3 days if kept in a refrigerator. Fish presented for sale without refrigeration should be discarded if unsold at the end of a day's trading.

Alteration of the chemical and microbiological composition of fish by the addition of enough salt or acetic acid can make the fish completely safe but the high concentreation required would not be acceptable to most consumers. However, a pH level of 4.5 in marinated products or a salt concentration of 3.0 per cent in smoked fish products is usually acceptable and affords added protection and extension of refrigerated shelf life. ●

Beware of gifts

If you don't wish to offend people who offer gifts of canned fish, be sure never to taste it until it has been thoroughly heated. It is fortunate that the botulism toxin is easily **heat** destroyed. (See advisory from Torry Research Station).

Chapter **35**

Safe canning methods

It cannot be emphasized too strongly that fish *must be canned in a pressure canner. No other method* can, for certain, destroy botulism spores if they are present. The *unsafe* methods include boiling water bath and oven canning. For example, the boiling water bath can only heat food to a temperature equal to the boiling point of water -212° F (100° C) at sea level. To kill the spores that cause botulism, food *must be heated to 240°F (118°C). Only a pressure canner can accomplish this.*

Pressure Canning Time Critical

For the pressure canner to bring the food up to the required, safe temperature, takes time. The heat must penetrate into the center of the pack. Every last bit of the food must reach 240° F (118° C) to be safe. The time necessary for fish to reach safe temperature has been determined by laboratories serving the commercial canning industry, and by government laboratories. The times given below are the *safe times.*

University of California
Cooperative Extension
United States Department of Agriculture

● TO CAN FISH

Be sure that the gauge on your pressure cooker has been tested for accuracy. Do not process for less than the prescribed time.

Use pint or smaller jars for canning fish. Wide mouth jars are easiest to fill. Or you can use small enamel-lined ½-pound or 1-pound tin cans.

Raw, Brine Pack

1. Use a knife that has a dull blade to scale salmon and other large-scaled fish. Scrape from tail to head. Skin tuna.
2. Remove fins and clean fish thoroughly. Cut off head and tail. Wash the body cavities thoroughly.
3. Split fish lengthwise along the backbone. Remove the backbone, leaving as little flesh on the bone as possible.
4. Cut fish into pieces the length of the jar or can. Soak pieces for 1 hour in a brine made of ½ pound (¾ cup) salt mixed in 1 gallon of water. (One gallon of brine is enough for about 25 pounds of cleaned fish.) Place a plate on the fish to keep it in the brine. Only use the brine once. Let the brined fish drain for several minutes.
   Alternate method. Fill the containers with pieces of fish as described in step 5. Add at least 1 teaspoon of salt and fill the jar or can with water.
5. Fill the jars or cans flush with the rim. Pack containers as full as possible with fish. Place the skin side of the fish next to the side of the container. Alternate head and tail ends if you are packing small fish. Do not add water if you soaked the fish in brine.
6. Seal jars. If you use cans, exhaust them in steam or in the oven because they are too shallow to set in hot water. If you use steam, leave the lids on. Seal after exhausting.
7. **Process at 10 pounds pressure, 240 °F for 1 hour and 50 minutes.**

To Can Smoked Fish

1. Can smoked fish immediately after smoking and cooling it. Cut fish into pieces the length of the jars or cans. Pack carefully.
2. **Seal and process according to directions for canning raw fish. Process 2 hours at 10 pounds pressure, 240 °F. ●**

● HOME CANNING OF FISH

Fish for canning must be strictly fresh.

The following directions are for the pressure cooker method. The boiling water bath and oven methods are not recommended.

Either glass sealers or tin cans may be used in pressure canning. Small (pint) sealers or 20 ounce cans are satisfactory. Wide mouth sealers are better than those with narrow tops, as the tender cooked fish is less likely to break when being removed for serving. If cans are used, the operating equipment must include a sealing machine.

Wash sealers thoroughly in hot soapy water and rinse in boiling water. Rinse cans in boiling water.

Prepare the fish by removing head, tail, fins and viscera. The backbone need not be removed, as it softens in the processing and its mineral content is valuable. The cleaned fish may be held for a few hours before canning, but must be stored in the coldest part of the refrigerator or packed in ice.

Cut fish in lengths to fit the containers and pack firmly, being careful not to break or crush the pieces. Leave ¼ inch space at top. Add ½ teaspoon salt to each container.

If sealers are used,

partly seal the filled containers and process them at the temperature and pressure indicated in the table below.

Follow manufacturer's directions for operating pressure cooker. Be sure to allow steam to flow freely from the petcock or vent for seven minutes to eliminate all air from the cooker. Then close petcock or vent and allow pressure to reach desired point. Start to count processing time when desired pressure or temperature is reached.

After processing the required time, remove cooker from heat and allow pressure to return gradually to zero.

Remove sealers, seal completely and cool in upright position. Label and store in a dark, cool place.

If tin cans are used,

put lids in place and complete the first sealing operation. Follow manufacturer's directions for operating sealing machine. Then place the cans in the pressure cooker and steam the cans for 15 minutes at 212° F. Leave the cover of the cooker unfastened.

Remove the cans from the cooker and immediately complete the sealing of the cans.

Return them to the cooker and process them at the temperature and pressure indicated in the table below.

Follow manufacturer's directions for operating pressure cooker. Be sure to allow steam to flow freely from the petcock or vent for seven minutes to eliminate all air. Then close petcock or vent and allow pressure to reach desired point. Start to count processing time when desired pressure or temperature is reached.

After processing the required time, remove cooker from heat and allow pressure to return gradually to zero.

Remove cans from cooker and cool quickly by immersing cans in cold water, changing the water so that they will cool rapidly. Dry thoroughly, label and store in a dry cool place.

Container	Fish	Processing Time Pressure
Glass Sealers "Small" (pint)	Salmon, Shad, etc.	110 mins. 10 lbs. (240° F)
Cans 20 oz. first crimping operation only		15 mins. to exhaust (212° F)
Then seal cans		100 mins. 10 lbs. (240° F)

Department of Fisheries of Canada. 1968. ●

A rule that is missing from both of the above advisories, but one that is closely followed by the commercial canning industry is: correct processing times are for *thawed* fish only - times do not apply to frozen fish - fish *must* be *thawed* before processing!

Pressure gauges

Pressure gauges are all we home canners have to guide us. The pressure gauge is only an indication of the temperature inside the canner (at 10 lbs. pressure the temperature is 240° F - 115° C). Commercial canners have thermometers as well as pressure gauges to show the internal temperature of their pressure cooking retorts. Accurate thermometers are too fragile for home use, however, so we must rely on our gauge being an accurate indication of temperature.

Gauges should be checked periodically to ensure their accuracy. The manufacturer of your canner can check your gauge for you. Your canner dealer may also know of a local service for gauges. The U.S. Department of Agriculture offers the following advice regarding gauges.

If the dial gauge is not acurate, tie a warning tag to the canner. On the tag, write the margin of error, the date the canner was tested, and the gauge setting to use for the correct presure (see below).

All directions in this bulletin require processing at 10 pounds of steam pressure. The following adjustments give the correct pressure:

If the gauge reads high—

1 pound high—process at 11 pounds.
2 pounds high—precces at 12 pounds.
3 pounds high—process at 13 pounds.
4 pounds high—process at 14 pounds.

If the gauge reads low—

1 pound low—process at 9 pounds.
2 pounds low—process at 8 pounds.
3 pounds low—process at 7 pounds.
4 pounds low—process at 6 pounds.

It is not safe to use a canner if the dial gauge registers as much as 5 pounds high or low. Replace a faulty gauge with an accurate one.

I am advised by the manufacturer of my Presto pressure canner that their weight type gauge requires no checking or recalibration. The instructions for using the canner include adjustment for canning at altitudes above sea level.

Following the above instructions to the letter is the *only* way you can assure the safety of your home canned fish. We all know people who use maverick canning methods, ones that deviate grossly from safe methods. Many who use unsafe canning methods do so in good faith, following old instructions written before botulism and the organisms that cause it were fully understood. Many speak of having *"Good luck"* with unsafe methods, not realising that they are playing *Russian Roulette.* It takes only one piece of bad luck to be fatal - perhaps to family and friends. The only bit of *good luck* such people are having is that there were no botulism spores in the fish they canned - next time that "luck" may run out!

USING A PRESSURE CANNER

Always follow the instructions provided by the manufacturer of your pressure canner. These rules are for your safety during the canning process and for the safety of the food after processing.

Glass Canning Jars

Always follow the instructions given by the manufacturer of your jars and the jar lids.

Metal Cans

To use metal cans you must have a can sealer. It is vital that you follow the instructions of the manufacturer of your sealer. Instruction concerning maintenance and adjustment are especially critical, because if not done with care, faulty seals can result. One of the most important operations in using metal cans is the seal testing. I speak from experience in these areas; once while changing can sizes, I hurried and apparently didn't take enough care in making adjustments. Coupled with the hurrying, I didn't use the correct testing technique. Later, cans began to swell from spoilage organisms getting in through poor seals, and many cans were lost. Fortunately the only loss was in fish, labor, and cans, and not in health. It was a good lesson for me.

Check sealing rolls frequently

A poor seal is found easily if cans are checked properly

Jars vs. Metal Cans

Metal cans for canning will give a better pack with some products, because fish packed in metal cans is cooled *immediately* after pressure cooking. Fish packed in glass jars is cooled *slowly* after pressure cooking. Some packs, such as smoked fish, and fish packed in sauce, suffer from flavor changes during long heating, (browning reaction). Glass jars must be cooled slowly to prevent their breaking, thus prolonging the heat process. Cans *must* be cooled quickly to complete the seal on the lids. Canning in glass jars is less expensive once the jars are acquired, but the saving may be lost if you give away some of your canned fish. Buying the can sealer adds to the higher *first cost* of using cans, but the *first cost* of jars gets higher each year too. In deciding on which way to go, you must simply consider your individual circumstances and preferences.

PRESERVING SMOKED FISH IN OIL

This method is akin to canning, but does not use heat to destroy spoilage organisms. Instead of using heat you protect the fish by immersing it in vegetable oil to exclude air then keeping it *refrigerated.*

By not using heat you do not alter the appearance or flavor of the *smoked* fish and have a more fresh-like product. I have kept *smoked* fish like this for a year.

Pack the sliced smoked fish in a sterilized canning jar, cover with oil, exclude air bubbles, and keep *refrigerated.*

Even a year later the product is still fresh-like.

6

SAUSAGES & SPECIALTY PRODUCTS

CONTENTS

Chapter **36**

Fish sausages

Contents

Sound like an odd title for a fish book? It does take a bit of getting used to. Fish is a fairly recent ingredient in the history of sausages, having been around less than 50 of the 5,000 years that meat sausages have. Even now, fish sausages enjoy popularity only in Japan, being little known elsewhere.

Japanese history shows that although fish loaves, known as Kamaboko, have been eaten for over 400 years, the fish sausage didn't make it in the marketplace until after World War II. Apparently fish sausage had made earlier bids for popularity, but success came only when Japan began to abandon the traditional rice diet after the war. Then fish sausage suddenly became a great phenomenon in Japanese food history. Japanese sausage manufacturers have even built huge manufacturing plants in a number of other countries and ship the products home to fill the demand. I can understand the popularity of fish sausages; I think they're excellent and think you may agree. Here's how to make them.

ABOUT SAUSAGE INGREDIENTS

Salt is an important ingredient because it extracts myosin from the fish protein which in turn forms a jell. This jell holds the ingredients in the sausage together when sliced or skinned. You can actually feel this phenomenon happening when you sprinkle salt on ground fish while kneading sausage ingredients together by hand.

Fat is an important but not totally essential ingredient. Fat (or oil) adds palatability, texture, and energy to the sausage. Pork fat is primarily used for fish as well as other sausages, and it is often diced into small *kernels* to contrast with the *emulsified* texture that fish tends to give to sausage. If you are saturated-fat conscious you can substitute vegetable oil for palatability and energy, or do without fat altogether.

Starch is important as an extender for the fish and also as a binder for the ingredients. You can use it in the form of either pure starch or flour, pure starch being a superior binder. Powdered milk may also be used.

Bread crumbs and cooked rice are also often used as sausage ingredients for the flavor and texture they lend. You can toast the bread crumbs for better flavor and texture if you like.

Water is an important ingredient as an extender and to help form the jell that makes a successful sausage. It is usually added in the form of ice and ground with the other ingredients. Ice has the value of keeping the ingredients cool during grinding and mixing. More heat is generated than you would expect, expecially if you are using an electric grinder and/or mixer.

Spices, of course, are a must if a sausage is to be a tasty sausage. Add the amount and kind of spices to suit *your* taste. On the subject of spices: I will give a number of typical ethnic formulas as examples. From them you can concoct your own formulas.

Ingredients usually follow these general proportions:

	Parts
Fish	66 to 93.5
Salt	1 to 3
Fat or oil	0 to 10
Starch	5 to 10
Breadcrumbs	0 to 5
Cooked rice	0 to 5
Spice mix	.5 to 1
Water	5 to 10

Spice Formulas

English

	10 lbs.	Sausage	5 kg	
garlic salt	.5	oz. 1 tbs.	15.5 g	15.0 ml
corriander	.3	oz. 1¼ tsp.	9.5 g	6.5 ml
pepper	.15	oz. ¾ tbs.	5.0 g	13.5 ml

German

white pepper	.4	oz. 2 tbs.	12.5 g	36.0 ml
nutmeg	.1	oz. 1½ tsp.	.3 g	8.0 ml
garlic powder	.025	oz. ½ tsp.	.75 g	2.5 ml

French

sugar	1.6	oz. 3½ tbs.	50.0 g	52.0 ml
black pepper	.6	oz. 3 tbs.	19.0 g	45.0 ml

Japanese

pepper	garlic	mustard
nutmeg	sage	mace
cardamon	clove	allspice
cinnamon	onion	msg

American

	10 lbs		Sausage	5 kg	
white pepper	.5	oz. 2¼ tbs.		15.5 g	45.0 ml
sugar	.42	oz. 2½ tsp.		12.5 g	12.5 ml
sage	.2	oz. 1 tbs.		6.0 g	15.0 ml
mace or nutmeg	.1	oz. 1½ tsp.		3.0 g	8.0 ml
ginger	.05	oz. ½ tsp.		1.5 g	3.0 ml

Canadian

corn flour	.3	oz. 1½ tbs.		9.5 g	23.0 ml
white pepper	.4	oz. 2 tbs.		12.5 g	36.0 ml
nutmeg or mace	.1	oz. 1½ tsp.		3.0 g	8.0 ml
thyme	.05 oz.	½ tsp.		1.5 g	2.5 ml
sage	.05 oz.	¾ tsp.		1.5 g	3.0 ml
sugar	.8	oz. 5 tsp.		23.0 g	25.0 ml

Chinese

sugar	1.6	oz. 3½ tbs.		50.0 g	50.0 ml
soy	.4	oz. 1 tbs.		12.5 g	15.0 ml
cinnamon	.1	oz. ¾ tbs.		3.0 g	3.0 ml

Italian

white pepper	.4	oz. 2 tbs.		12.5 g	36.0 ml
fennel	.4	oz. 1¾ tbs.		12.5 g	36.0 ml
mild red pepper	.4	oz. 2 tbs.		12.5 g	36.0 ml
corriander	.2	oz. ¾ tsp.		6.0 g	4.0 ml
paprika	.2	oz. 1¼ tsp.		6.0 g	6.0 ml

Polish

corn syrup	2.4	oz. 3½ tbs.		75.0 g	54.0 ml
black pepper	.2	oz. 1 tbs.		6.0 g	15.0 ml
marjoram	.1	oz. 1½ tsp.		3.0 g	7.5 ml
garlic powder	.025 oz.	½ tsp.		.75 g	2.5 ml

MAKING THE SAUSAGE

1. Skin fillets

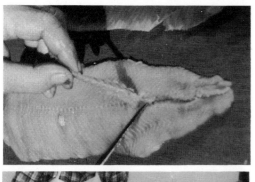

2. Bone

3. Grind fish and ice together (fine plate)

4. Chop fat (coarse plate)

5. Grind breadcrumbs (fine)

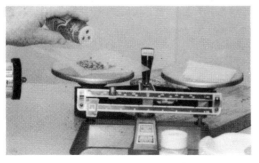

6. Weigh or measure spices

7. Mix dry ingredients together

8. Mix wet and dry ingredients together thoroughly

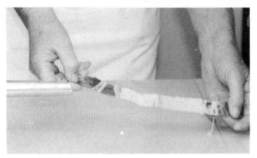

9. Artificial casings come ready to slip on the horn

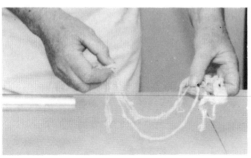

10. If you store your natural casings salted, and/or frozen, thaw and freshen them just before using and keep them wet. They will look like an unmanagable mess, but don't worry about them.

11. Straighten the casings out by blowing the twists out to start.

12. Once started on the stuffing horn, the casing can be untwisted easily. Feed as much casing on the horn as you will need, or as much as you can at one time.

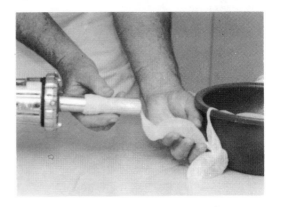

13. Tie off the end after you have stuffed the first 6 inches, then stuff allowing the casing to slip off the horn when it is moderately packed. Don't pack too tightly, so that you can link the sausages without bursting the casing.

14. Link by twisting.

After linking, sausages may or may not be cooked; it will depend on the type and how they are used. Sausages that are intended for frying, e.g. breakfast sausages, may be fried immediately or frozen or canned for future use.

Most people prefer sausages cooked in a smoker or at least partially so. You can, however, cook them in water; some commercial sausages are cooked this way. In either case, the cooking time will depend again on the type - how it will be used, e.g. wieners that are intended to be heated before use are only partially cooked during processing. Sausages that are to be sliced for eating cold must be *thoroughly* cooked during processing.

Water cooking

Don't let the cooking water exceed 190° F (90° C) else the sausages will burst.

	Time
Breakfast sausages	none if desired
Wieners ¾ in (20 mm)	30 min.
Large links 1¾ in (45 mm)	1 hr.
Slicing sausage 1¾ in (45 mm)	1 hr.

Sausages draped on smoke-stick for smoking.

Smoke cooking

Smoke temperature	140° F (60° C
Breakfast ¾ in. (20 mm)	3½ hrs.
Wieners ¾ in. (20 mm)	3½ hrs.
Large links 1¾ in. (45 mm)	5 hrs.
Slicing sausage 3¼ in. (80 mm)	6½ hrs.

Sausages shrink during smoking.

Post smoking treatment

Hot water *not* to exceed 190° F (90° C)

	Hot Water	Ice Water
Breakfast sausages ¾ in. (20 mm)	3 min.	3 min.
Wieners ¾ in. (20 mm)	3 min.	3 min.
Large links 1¾ in. (45 mm)	30 min.	1 hr.
Slicing sausage 3¼ in. (80 mm)	1 hr.	1½ hr.

A brief treatment in hot water plumps smoked sausages.

Sausages in natural casings are not usually skinned before using or freezing, but you can skin linked sausages in artificial casings, before further cooking or freezing. They should be firm and hold together well after the foregoing treatments, because the heat has coagulated the protein of the fish.

Finished product ready for freezing.

Freezing or canning sausages

You should quick freeze raw sausages (see definition, chapter 31) as you would any fresh fish. Cooked or partially cooked sausages are not as critical and can stand to be only fast frozen. Any fish product must be stored below 0° F (-18° C) and will have a better freezer life and eating quality if you can keep it at -20° F (-29° C).

You may can sausages in light brine - 1 tsp. (5 ml) salt to 1 pint (500 ml) water.

If you wish to can smaller sized sausages, plan ahead because the canning intensifies smoke, spice and herb flavorings. Don't make highly spiced and smoked sausages, then decide to can them.

Use ½ to ⅔ the amount of flavoring and ⅔ the smoking time. *Do not* include sage in the spice formula - it will become bitter after canning.

Follow instruction given for canning fish in chapter 35.

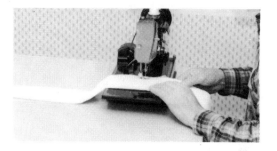

MAKING SLICING SAUSAGE

1. Muslin makes an excellent sausage casing. I use an 8 in. (200 mm) strip, folded in half and stitched to form a tube.

2. Turn the seam to the inside.

3. Tie off the end and stuff.

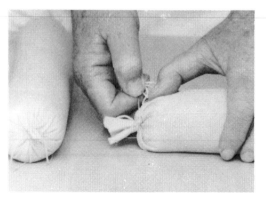

4. Then tie off the other end.
5. Follow instruction given above for smoking, cooking and cooling.

Chapter **37**

Fish Hams, Bacons, and other specialties

I call this product "Bacon" because it is cured and smoked like bacon, and is an excellent substitute for bacon, having, if anything more uses than the original.

This is a cold smoked product, so to make it, you must have a smoker that is capable of cold smoking.

You can best make the product from a thickish fillet (see filleting chapter 3) which you have completely boned. If you don't want to bone the fillet before curing you can also do a good job of boning as you cut slices off the cured and smoked fillet for frying, etc.

Bacon, step 1

Make a curing brine:

water	80 oz	2 l
pickling salt	4.6 oz	130 g
*sugar (white or brown)	4.8 oz.	135 g
pickling spices 1 tbs.	15 ml	

You may use less sugar to your taste.

When the salt and sugar have dissolved, *simmer* pickling spices in a cup of the brine for 15 minutes.

brine	1 cup	250 ml
mixed pickling spices	1 tbs	15 ml

Cool the spice-brine mix and add the rest of the brine, cool the mix to 40° F (5° C).

Cure the fillets according to thickness

¾ in.	6 hrs.
1 in.	8 hrs.
1½ in.	10 hrs.
2 in.	15 hrs.
3 in.	20 hrs.

Freshen the fillets after curing. Drain them of brine and freshen in cold running water:

¾ in.	15 min.
1 in.	20 min.
1½ in.	30 min.
2 in.	45 min.
3 in.	60 min.

Drain the fillets well on the smoking racks before placing in the smoker.

Step 2

The balance of the process consists of smoking, then further drying in the smoker - *without smoke* or with as little as possible.

Smoking

Smoke temperature	85° F (30° C)	
Smoke density	Forced draft - medium,	Natural draft - light

Smoking times

	Forced draft smoker	Natural draft smoker
¾ in.	4 hrs.	*up to 8 hrs.
1 in.	5 hrs.	*up to 10 hrs.
1½ in.	7 hrs.	*up to 14 hrs.
2 in.	10 hrs.	*up to 20 hrs.
3 in.	12 hrs.	*up to 24 hrs.

*Time depends on the outside temperature and amount of smoke circulation. See chapter 6.

Drying temp.	85° F	30° C
Smoke	Forced draft	none
	Natural draft	use a small clear fire to get air circulation with as little smoke as possible

Drying times

	Forced draft	Natural draft
¾ in.	2 hrs.	*up to 4 hrs.
1 in.	2½ hrs.	*up to 5 hrs.
1½ in.	4 hrs.	*up to 8 hrs.
2 in.	6 hrs.	*up to 12 hrs.
3 in.	8 hrs.	*up to 16 hrs.

*See smoking times.

After smoking, cool the fillets to refrigerator temperature before wrapping; a day in the frig will make them easier to slice.

Slice the bacon before freezing if you wish, or freeze the fillet whole. It will keep better in the freezer if you freeze the whole fillet, then glaze and seal in moisture proof wrap: e.g. plastic bag.

"Bacon" will keep in the frig for about the same length of time as pork or beef bacon.

Using "Bacon"

Slice the cured fillet about ¼ in. (6 mm) thick; any thinner slices are harder to cook.

You can either pan or deep-fat fry the strips.

Bacon strips make an excellent breakfast dish.

Bacon can be cooked enough to crumble then used in any number of dishes: creamed, added to cooked vegetables, in salads, and as a pizza dressing.

FISH HAMS

I know it's difficult to conjure up a vision of a fish with a haunch like a pig - so how to explain "Fish Ham"?

Fish ham is really a fish loaf. Such items are unheard of anywhere but in Japan. There they have been popular for hundreds of years. The Japanese call these loaves *Kamaboko* which translates something like fish jelly. I suppose such a translation is natural because of the *jelled* nature the loaf takes on when cooked. The loaf jells, partly because it contains pickled or cured fish as well as fresh fish.

To describe such a product as Kamaboko in North America, translators borrow from the Meat Trade and describe the loaf as a "Ham". In North America there are "Turkey Hams" as well as "Ham Hams". The Trade uses this expression because part of the Turkey Ham is cured like a pork ham is.

At any rate, the fish *ham* for which I'll give the formula, has been enthusiastically received by everyone we've served it to.

• How to make Fish "Ham"

Two pounds of fish, along with the other ingredients makes a loaf that will fill a 8½ × 4½ × 2½ in. loaf pan.

For the *cured* fish use Pickled-Smoked from chapter 14.

1 lb. raw fish 450 g	⅓ cup breadcrumbs 80 ml
1 lb. pickled smoked fish 450 g	⅓ cup wheatlets or cream of of wheat 80 ml
2 oz. vegetable oil 60 ml	¾ cup cooked rice 180 ml

Eggs are optional; they help bind the loaf.

Add enough water or wine to get a mix that will pack tightly enough for thin slicing.

You may want to add some of the seasonings used in sausages, but if you do keep in mind that the Pickled Smoked fish is already flavored by pickling spices. Go easy on adding more spices the first time.

Making the loaf

1. Bone and skin the fish.

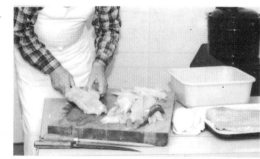

2. Grind the fish-fine plate if you want thin slices.

3. Add the dry ingredients to the fish and knead together adding the egg and liquid to get a mass that will stick together.
4. Pack well into a well greased loaf pan.
5. Cook in a preheated 350° F oven for 45 to 60 minutes or until loaf is firm.

6. The "Ham" may be served hot or cold. It makes an excellent cold luncheon or sandwich slice, and is very tasty as a hot appetizer. Also great fried with eggs for breakfast; in short, use anyway you would use a smoked ham.

FISH STICKS

Most North Americans are familiar with fish sticks, but not with how to make them. It's quite simple, but to make it worth while you may want to make a big batch for freezing for quick family meals.

The sticks may be made from unsmoked or a combination of smoked and unsmoked fish. It is best not to use too much smoked fish in any of these specialties because it doesn't have quite the ability to bind that unsmoked has.

1 lb. skinned & boned fillets 450 g	*2 tbs. instant blending flour 30 ml*
4½ oz. milk 135 ml	*¾ tsp. salt 3 ml*
5 tbs. bread crumbs 75 ml	*herbs or spices to suit*

1. Skin and bone fillets.
2. Grind through the fine plate.
3. Blend all ingredients together thoroughly.
4. Spred on *oiled* trays, cookie sheets or similar, a layer ½ in. (12 mm) thick.

5. Freeze until mixture is semi hard - about 30 minutes.
6. Cut slab into strips, then into sticks.
7. Freeze thoroughly.

8. Dip frozen sticks quickly in milk then into bread or cracker crumbs, package and immediately put back into freezer.

9. To serve, either fry the frozen sticks in a small amount of oil or place in a preheated 400° F (205° C) oven for 8 to 10 minutes.

FISH CRISPS

This is a party item that can be made from smoked or unsmoked fish or a combination of the two. The crisps are best made ahead of time then frozen for occasions. When ready to use, take them from the freezer, drop them into the deep fat fryer at 390° F (200° C), fry a few minutes until brown, and serve.

1 lb. skinned & boned fillets 450 g	2½ tbs. starch (corn or potato) 45 ml
2 cups *water 120 ml	¾ tsp. salt 3 ml
2½ tbs. dried potato flakes 45 ml	garlic or other flavoring to taste

1. Skin and bone the fillets
2. Grind the fish through the finest plate.
3. Mix well with the other ingredients * adding or deleting water to get a mixture that will extrude easily from a pastry tube—not too thin, though.
4. If you don't have a pastry tube, cut the corner off a plastic freezer bag and use it to extrude that paste into the deep fryer at 390° F (200° C). Don't extrude too much into the fat at one time; too much paste will cool the fat. You want to cook it only for 2 to 3 seconds before freezing and the fat must stay hot.
5. Place the hot crisp on paper towels to blot off fat and cool.
6. Cut into individual crisps and freeze immediately.
7. To serve, fry at 390° F (200° C) until brown, and serve hot.

FISH PUFFS

Here is a sure winner at parties. The process is a bit longer than that of some of the other appetizers, but the results are certainly worth the effort.

Commercial producers of products like this have a special starch available to them - high amylopectin starch, from waxy corn or sorghum - that makes a really puffy product. We at home, however, must be satisfied with ordinary corn, potato, or rice starch.

Ingredients

1 lb. boned & skinned fillets 450 g	2 tbs. salt 30 ml
2 2/3 cups corn starch 640 ml	1 tbs. sugar 13 ml
3½ oz. water 105 ml	

1. Grind the fillets extra fine or preferably blend them.
2. Mix the fish with the other ingredients, preferably with an electric mixer, reserving a little of the water. Mix thoroughly with enough water to get a paste that comes away from the bowl cleanly.

3. Pack the paste into half pint tapered canning jars and seal.

4. Cook the jars in a covered steamer, at no pressure for 3 hours.

5. Cool the jars and refrigerate for at least 48 hours. Then unmold and slice the roll as thinly as possible.

6. Dry the slices at lowest heat in the oven, or in your dehydrator. I dry and smoke mine in my forced-draft smoker at 100° F (40° C).

7. You can store the thoroughly dried chips at room temperature if you seal them from the air.

8. When ready to entertain, drop the chips into hot oil at 390° F (200° C) for a few seconds. Watch them puff as they brown!

9. Serve them proudly.

SMOKED FISH PASTE

One of the more elegant ways of using smoked fish is in a paste. The paste traditionally is made with butter, but if you can't stand for it being so sinfully delicious, you can use margarine, cream cheese, or cottage cheese to cut down on the fat.

Butter	81% fat (animal)
Margarine	80% (vegetable)
Cream Cheese	37% (animal)
Skim Cottage Cheese	0.5%

To make the paste, weigh out equal weights of the smoked fish and the butter or it's substitute. Use either a mortar and pestle, blender or food processor to reduce the fish to a pulp, blend in the butter, then season with lemon juice and perhaps a bit of cayenne for spirit.

The paste can be kept in the fridge for a year if the container is kept sealed with clarified butter after each use; (there is no substitute for butter in this).

There are many ways that you can use smoked fish paste: on crackers or toast, on steaks or slices of meat, or on eggs, to name a few.

BRINE TABLE

% Salinometer	For 4 qts.	For 4 liters
10	3.6 oz.	114 g
20	7.2	228
30	11.2	352
40	15.4	486
50	19.8	622
60	24.4	770
70	29.4	926
80	34.6	1090
90	40.4	1272
100	46.6	1468

From page 41

Brine pumping needles can be ordered through your hardware store, can be found at butcher supply houses, are often carried by custom butchering shops, and catalogue supply houses. I ordered mine from Morton Salt Co. many years ago.